AF254855

A NONPROFIT LEADER'S EDGE

by

Mike B. Logan

A Nonprofit Leader's Edge
Copyright © 2026 by Mike B. Logan

Cover art by Andrew Montesi
Sigmoid chart graphics used with permission from the Author.

For information, contact Mike B. Logan
3506 Wasatch Drive, Redding, CA 96001

ISBN 979-8-218-94226-7

Printed in USA by 48HrBooks (www.48HrBooks.com)

PRAISE FOR MIKE LOGAN'S BOOK

"I thoroughly enjoyed reading *A Non-Profit Leader's Edge* by Mike Logan.

"The book was insightful and full of inspiration and practical ideas about leadership during the challenging times we are currently experiencing. I especially appreciated Mike's personal stories of trials and triumphs. He was not afraid to talk about moments when he might have done or said the wrong thing as a leader, and he consistently highlighted the lessons he learned from those experiences.

"The section on leading with compassion particularly hit home for me. I tend to rely too heavily on compassion in my leadership style, and in the past that has sometimes led to negative effects for both me and my team. I appreciated Mike naming this so directly, especially because our culture often leans toward compassion in every situation—when sometimes it may not be the most appropriate response.

"Thank you, Mike, for such an inspirational and thought-provoking read!

Lianne Richelieu, CEO
College and Career Options Inc.

"In *A Nonprofit Leader's Edge*, Mike Logan draws on his extensive leadership experience to deliver a practical, actionable guide for sharpening your leadership skills and elevating your organization. Beyond building robust systems and cultivating clear, open communication, Logan emphasizes one of the book's most powerful themes: developing leaders who can solve problems and think independently.

"This book is packed with valuable insight from start to finish."

Michael Flinders
Board Member

"*A Nonprofit Leaders Edge* is the kind of book every nonprofit leader wishes they had five years earlier. Mike Logan brings uncommon clarity to the challenges we face, designing the future, building thinking teams, leading with principles, and creating organizations that scale. It reads like practical leadership coaching from someone who has lived the work. Any executive, new or seasoned, will walk away more focused, more capable, and more prepared to lead."

Jonathan Anderson
CEO and Executive Director
Good News Rescue Mission

"I'm grateful that Mike has written *A Nonprofit Leader's Edge* - the nonprofit sector needs his wisdom, and so does the world.

"Mike is a rare leader who makes commercial, social and personal impact, having done so for many years. The book reflects who Mike is — pragmatic, no nonsense, innovative and impactful. His words come with the authority of a man who has walked out every insight on the pages.

"I've benefited from Mike's mentorship in recent years and I'm glad that you now get to as well!"

Andrew Montesi, Founder
Apiro Marketing and The Montesi Company

"I wish Mike Logan's new book, *A Nonprofit Leader's Edge,* had been on my desk 30 years ago as a necessary reference as I started managing nonprofit organizations.

"Mike Logan condenses his 40 years of experience in leading nonprofits to success in this inspiring new book.

"Mike draws from his successful career numerous practical suggestions for solving everyday problems that arise in the nonprofit world. In problem solving, leadership challenges, or strategic planning, knowing what critical questions to ask is key to moving forward a successful organization. This innovative book lays out a plethora of issues related to nonprofit supervisors that give the reader the appropriate questions to pursue.

"I strongly recommend this book to every nonprofit leadership team in the United States, Europe and Asia as required reading to assist them in meeting their organizational goals and objectives.

"Mike Logan's new book is a significant contribution to advancing leadership skills with everyday problems and challenges in nonprofit organizations.'

Jim Milestone
Retired Superintendent,
US National Park Service

"Reading *A Nonprofit Leader's Edge* reinforced the value of leading with long-term vision, personal responsibility, and intentional systems.

"Mike brings decades of experience building organizations and developing leaders who can carry a mission forward through change.

"In an increasingly complex nonprofit landscape, this book offers enduring principles that challenge leaders to move beyond reaction and thoughtfully design organizations built to last.

"I was especially struck by the consistent focus on long-term vision, personal responsibility, and building systems and leaders that can carry the mission forward through change.

"In a world where nonprofit leadership can feel very reactive, your perspective on intentionally designing the future felt both grounding and timely."

Shannon Pierce, CEO
Executive Director

"This book is a powerful guide for nonprofit leaders seeking both inspiration and practical direction. It blends timeless wisdom with actionable strategies that address today's real-world challenges.

"Clear, insightful, and grounded in real experience, it equips leaders with the knowledge needed to build resilient organizations and achieve sustainable, mission-driven growth."

Winston Hernandez

"Wow! Mike, your book is full of helpful and even vital information for anyone engaged in the nonprofit world. It would be hard to imagine a book out there with the same level of helpful information.

"Great job!"

Doug Shelton
LMFT

"Mike Logan is the most innovative non-profit leader I have ever met.

"He stays well informed about trends that will impact his organization and he reacts to them not just simply observing them and hoping for the best.

"In *A Nonprofit Leader's Edge*, he shares his wisdom and insight gained over decades of leading organizations and teams. This book will help you become a better leader and will help your organization serve its 218 constituents with excellence!!"

Brad Williams
Director of Services
Former college CFO
Nonprofit founder
Community leader

"*A Nonprofit Leader's Edge* distills 40 years of lived experience into clear, actionable wisdom for today's leaders.

"Mike Logan combines systems thinking, principled leadership, and practical storytelling to show how clarity, curiosity, and well-designed processes transform organizations.

"Read through a modern lens of operations, quality and project management, his insights become a blueprint for building resilient teams, simplifying complexity, strengthening culture, and leading with integrity — all while keeping mission, people and future impact at the center."

Henry Whitlow
MBA, Harvard University
Adjunct Professor at
Clark School of Business

"Mike Logan's *Straight Talk* section is a gift to nonprofit leaders hungry for honesty and clarity.

"His candid insights cut through jargon and bravely name the tough dynamics boards and executives often tiptoe around.

"The practical wisdom in these pages helps leaders build trust, face hard truths, and make better decisions — strengthening both organizational culture and long term impact for the communities and people they serve."

Gordon Flinn
President/CEO and Founder
of GoForth Consulting

"Mike Logan's *A Nonprofit Leader's Edge* is a powerful testament to his commitment to cutting-edge leadership and the belief that great leaders must always look forward.

"His approach challenges nonprofit executives to measure both their successes and failures with honesty, courage, and purpose — then lead from the front with clarity and conviction.

"What makes this book truly special is Mike himself: a dedicated servant-leader whose heart for the Northern California communities he serves is unmistakable and whose passion for helping youth become the very best version of themselves shines through every page.

"This is more than a leadership guide — it's a reflection of Mike's lifelong mission to elevate others."

Greg Howard
CEO/Founder
One Family Athletics

"What Mike Logan shares in this book is far more than leadership advice, it is hard-earned wisdom rooted in integrity, compassion and courage. His perspective challenges leaders to elevate their thinking, invest in people, and design the future with purpose. Reading this book feels like sitting with a trusted mentor. It will strengthen not only your organization, but your character as a leader."

Matt Williams
School Counselor,
Foster Parent

"Leadership is like building a cathedral: vision serves as the soaring blueprint that guides every decision, culture forms the solid foundation supporting the entire structure, and systems are the intricate arches and vaults that hold it all aloft.

"*A Nonprofit Leader's Edge* equips nonprofit leaders to design organizations that are both resilient and inspiring.

"Mike Logan truly lives this legacy, balancing compassion with accountability, fostering innovation, and nurturing talent like master builders preparing future generations.

"Just as a cathedral requires careful planning, skilled craftsmanship, and attention to both detail and grandeur, effective nonprofit leadership demands foresight, ethical integrity, strategic systems and a culture that elevates every individual.

"Through listening, mentoring and modeling growth, Mike Logan demonstrates how nonprofits can rise beyond immediate challenges to create lasting impact that stands the test of time.

Haydee Chang
CEO Trilogy

"This book stands out for its honesty, clarity, and genuine relevance to real-world situations. It does not rely on theory alone but speaks directly to the daily pressure leaders face and the responsibility they carry. The balance of urgency, wisdom, and practical leadership makes this book leaders will return to often.

"*A Nonprofit Leader's Edge* offers a grounded, experience-driven look at leadership that goes beyond theory and into lived reality. It challenges readers to think deeply about responsibility, courage, alignment and foresight while remaining practical and accessible.

"Mike Logan blends hard-earned lessons with clear frameworks, making this a valuable guide for leaders who want to build resilient organizations and grow personally without losing integrity or purpose.

"What makes this book compelling is its honesty.

"It does not romanticize leadership or offer quick fixes. Instead, it presents leadership as a disciplined practice requiring clarity, accountability and the willingness to sit with discomfort.

"The insights feel earned rather than academic, making the guidance especially relevant for nonprofit and mission-driven leaders navigating complexity, change, and human dynamics in real time."

Joey Hughes
Director of Programs
Good News Rescue Mission

"Having worked alongside Mike Logan for two decades, I witnessed leadership rooted in integrity, vision, and an unwavering commitment to service.

"His ability to build, expand, and sustain multiple nonprofit divisions -- while consistently centering mission and people -- is rare and sets him apart. This book reflects the same steady, values-driven leadership that shaped Mike's organization, empowered countless professionals, and achieved "changed lives" for children and families.

"Mike's insights are practical, principled, and deeply earned.

Delrae Hansen
Chief Program Officer

TESTIMONIAL

"A Nonprofit Leader's Edge" is a rare gift to the field of leadership — the kind of book which emerges only from decades of lived experience, disciplined reflection and a genuine love for people.

Mike Logan writes with the clarity of a seasoned executive, the courage of a founder who weathered every storm and the heart of a servant leader committed to elevating others. His insights are not theoretical; they are forged in real crises, real decisions and real communities. What he offers in these pages is both refreshingly practical and deeply principled.

Mike Logan understands something critical: Leadership is not about ego — it is about stewardship, systems and the long horizon of impact. His emphasis on curiosity, values, clarity of purpose and the design of simple yet powerful systems aligns with the very best traditions of organizational excellence. His ability to turn adversity into wisdom will encourage every leader who ever felt alone under the weight of responsibility.

I enjoyed the privilege of coaching leaders across industries for many years. However, Mike Logan's work stands out because it combines strategy with soul. He reminds us great leadership is not accidental — it is intentional, disciplined and rooted in service. His journey proves when leaders invests in their people, aligns decision making with core principles and keeps a long view of the future, then entire communities will flourish.

This book will strengthen emerging leaders and re-ignite veteran executives. It is an invitation to lead with vision, integrity and courage — and to build organizations capable of changing lives for generations.

I enthusiastically recommend *"A Nonprofit Leader's Edge"* to anyone committed to leading with wisdom and creating a lasting legacy of impact.

Henry Whitlow
Executive Coach • Business Architect • Professor
and Co-Founder of MDP American Freedom Initiative

DEDICATION

To my wife Terri,
my children and
my grandchildren.

ACKNOWLEDGEMENTS

People who helped edit this book:
In appreciation of George Lawrence Winship
who guided me through the editing process.
Roman Sahagun
Monte Montesi
Without these people, *A Nonprofit Leader's Edge*
would neither be attempted nor completed!

PEOPLE WHO ENCOURAGED ME

I want to especially thank those who reviewed my book:

Reviewers:

Henry Whitlow
Lianne Richelieu
Michael Flinders
Jonathan Anderson
Andrew Montesi
Jim Milestone
Shannon Pierce
Winston Hernandez
Doug Shelton
Brad Williams
Matt Williams
Greg Howard
Gordon Flinn
Haydee Chang
Joey Hughes
Delrae Hansen

FORWARD

Throughout my career, I have dedicated myself to nonprofit leadership, guiding organizations that span diverse areas such as group homes, foster care, substance abuse recovery, domestic violence treatment, church pastoring, and even founding a global family strengthening organization. It is in these nonprofit settings that I cultivated my leadership skills. A pivotal figure in my journey has been Mike Logan, whose influence and mentorship were instrumental in my early development.

Mike became my supervisor during my first nonprofit role at Remi Vista, an organization that integrated group home care for juvenile offenders, foster care, and a counseling center staffed with licensed therapists. This multifaceted organization provided me with invaluable experiences as I entered the social services arena. At the time, I was finishing my Bachelor's degree at Chico State, and Mike took me under his wing, nurturing my growth as a young manager at just 28 years old.

I cherish the memories of Mike imparting essential leadership principles and introducing me to influential authors. During this formative period, I immersed myself in the works of Stephen Covey, Peter Drucker, John Maxwell, The Arbinger Group, Jim Collins, and many others. Much of my foundational leadership development occurred during those years of mentorship. Through our discussions, I learned to identify priorities and execute actions strategically. Mike also taught me how to manage stress effectively and find fulfillment in my role as a leader—the fruits of his mentorship have had a lasting impact on my life.

In many ways, Mike's book, A Nonprofit Leader's Edge, serves as a similar opportunity for readers. It distills the cumulative wisdom he has gained from years of study and practice, making it accessible at your fingertips. At his core, Mike is a developer of people; John Maxwell would categorize him as a "Level 5 Leader." He surrounds himself with capable, competent individuals who, in turn, develop those around them, creating a culture of leadership growth.

While it may be tempting for leaders to surround themselves with followers, such an approach is limiting. True legacy-building leaders understand the importance and value of cultivating depth within their teams. By helping team members see the vision clearly, leaders can instill an understanding of the sacrifices required for the marathon ahead. Teaching your people to embrace truth, communicate authentically, care for one another, and protect relationships is essential for building long-term trust and achieving great results.

I am genuinely excited for you to explore the pages of this book, as I am certain of the profound impact Mike has had on my life—and I believe it will resonate with you as well.

Danny Silk
Founder of Loving On Purpose
Author of: *Keep Your Love On,*
Culture of Honor
and *The Way of the Dragon Slayer*

TABLE OF CONTENTS

LEADERSHIP REQUIRES A LONG VIEW
OF THE HORIZON

"The only limit to our realization of tomorrow
will be our doubts of today."

Franklin D. Roosevelt

"Vision without action is merely a dream.
Action without vision just passes the time.
Vision with action can change the world."

Joel A. Barker

"Leadership is the capacity to translate vision into reality."

Warren Bennis

"What you get by achieving your goals
is not as important as what you become
by achieving your goals."

Zig Ziglar

As a leader, how can you transform your agency in the next three years? How can you decide today which daily tasks will best create the future you want for your organization?

In order to answer those questions, a leader needs some concept of the future he or she desires to create. Remember, knowing what you want to accomplish and what your future will be is based entirely on the actions you take today and every day going forward.

The longer your horizon, the more precise your decisions will be and the less anxiety you will have about your choices. Whether you have a short vision or long vision of life, it impacts every aspect of your existence. When you decide what you want your future to look like, you can then take the necessary actions to create this future. For a leader, the benefit of long-term thinking and planning is to help you overcome obstacles and daily problems with more peace. You will also maintain a better perspective of the things happening in your own life.

Recently I shared a conversation with a young man whom I mentored. Because I knew he was a planner and set some ambitious goals for life, I was interested in how he saw his own future.

What impressed me about my friend was this: He and his fiancé held such a long view of their future life together. Before they were betrothed, they discussed children and finances. He was raised in a poor family. Therefore, he wanted to create a great life for his wife and family. They started out life together from the perspective of where they both wanted to be 30 years later. They met with a financial advisor and took the actions necessary to set up a savings and investment plan. They wanted a plan, a vision of what their future should look like, so they could take the necessary steps to get where they wanted to be at each stage of their lives together.

This is the same thing great leaders do. They have a plan; they seek guidance; they create action around their plans and then stay aware of when they are on track as well as when they fall off.

Leaders must invest in their own future. You invested in this book because you want your future to be created by you, not by random events. I want you to have the wisdom and tactics I learned the hard way, through experience. I want you to obtain peace and confidence in being a leader, not feeling harassed and intimidated by the uncontrollable events surrounding you.

When you finish this book, you will have more skills and more knowledge about leadership because I want you to know everything I learned after 40 years of leadership in non-profit organizations, both in starting several as well as taking over failing organizations and turning them around. Therefore, I can support you in your leadership journey by walking with you through the challenges of leadership.

You won't need to walk through your time of leadership alone wondering whether you'll ever get out of your current situation. With the knowledge provided in this book, you will summit more joyous mountain tops and suffer fewer emotional valleys. You'll learn how to reduce friction with your employees. You'll make a positive impact on your community and feel great about what you do.

Most people spend so little time thinking about the future!

What I want for you is to think more about your future while handling your present situation powerfully, not by looking askance at any setbacks you may suffer.

At various times, all leaders experience the following:
- Fear
- Anxiety
- Chaos
- Lack of being connected to a larger network
- Lack of money and resources

Just know this, if a leader is experiencing the first two things on this list, they may be so restrained emotionally they won't have the strength to strategize, dream or even think about their organization's future.

Research shows us a leader won't be able to see far into their own future and make plans as well as implement those plans if they are struggling inside. Suffering through anxiety and fear will keep a leader from correcting items three through five.

Sometimes a leader in this dilemma can only think in terms of a 24-hour horizon. When they are in this much panic and stress, it usually requires some long-term planning and taking action to work their way through the issues. Without doing the proper amount of planning, they can often become stuck in this state. In such a scenario, a leader may not be able to make the appointments needed nor create the planning meetings to be aware of deadlines for filing the paperwork necessary for effective leadership.

My intention for this book is to assist leaders trapped in this condition to achieve a larger horizon. It is the only way they will ever have the life they all seek and want.

I recently realized I think more about the past than the future. Some might say I have spent more time in the past than I'll ever have in the future. While this may be true, then what is the value in looking backwards. If I haven't already received the valuable lessons from the past, there's probably not a lot I can do now to retrieve them.

Whatever your age, you have a future if you have faith in God. With God, you have a powerful partner. With God's help, you can create the world you want to live in. It is important for you to believe you have a long horizon for your own life and also for the life of your organization. We make better decisions when we have our future in the forefront of what we think, what we do and the actions we undertake!

Having your future in mind will also help you in making ethical and sound decisions in the present. Im reminded of an article titled Short Horizons and Tempting Situations: Lack of Continuity to Our Future Selves Leads to Unethical Decision Making and Behavior by Hershfield, Cohen and Thompson. Their research shows when we have a view of what we want our future to be, we are more likely to make strong ethical decisions and have a greater sense of peace whenever we face difficult choices.

I started the first Christian faith-based social model drug and alcohol treatment program in northern California. It was called The Good Shepherd. Our clients were men and women who were strung out on methamphetamine and heroin. They were financially, spiritually and emotional bankrupt and doing sordid things simply to obtain their drugs daily.

I soon became a resource for the treatment community. Jail personnel would telephone me occasionally and let me know when an inmate desired to talk with me. On one occasion, I responded to such a request. The call was from a young man who at one time was a prospect to be a professional baseball player. However, his abuse of drugs stole the opportunity away from him. After going through jailhouse security and being searched, he and I were led to a small room where we could speak privately without interference.

As we conversed, he repeatedly told me about how there were still a lot of drugs in his house. When he was arrested, the house where he stayed was searched. Apparently, the police only found part of his stash. He told me if I would retrieve his remaining drugs and deliver them to a contact of his, he would split the proceeds with me.

At first, I couldn't believe what he was suggesting.

He was headed for prison and I was managing a drug and alcohol recovery program. A faith-based one at that. I knew he was checking me out to see whether he could co-opt me to find his drugs and then take them to his connection.

Most likely he was unaware I needed to go out every month and raise $7,000 to $8,000 just to keep The Good Shepherd operating since there wasn't any treatment funding as there is now. I was always just one month away from having to close down my own program. As he continually mentioned the drugs, I found myself tempted to do what he was suggesting as a way to keep my program financially afloat. Talk about crazy!

Yes, I was tempted! For me, temptation means having an idea roll through my head more than once. However, I stayed true to my values and my faith. I sternly told the young man if he mentioned the drugs again, I would leave and not return. He did stop talking about the drugs and I was eventually able to help him resolve some of his other issues before he was sent to prison.

I guarantee, someday you will meet your future self. What will be your reaction? Will you be fulfilled or suffering from a sense of failure?

My desire is for you to stop and see your life from a point in the future. What do you want the future to look like for you? Now is the time for you to start thinking about what you want your future to be and decide what actions you need to take in order to get there.

Finding out who you want to be in the future and how you want your life to look like is the most powerful thing you can do! In three years or 20 years, will you be someone whom you admire? Will you be someone with a life full of achievements and at peace with great relationships?

Or not!

It is up to you.

When you understand clearly what you want your future self to be, you will move faster than you can imagine it is possible to create this future. Obviously, the organization you lead will also reflect who you are and who you want to become. Let your future self-guide the decisions you make today. Let your future self-decide what kind of character you will have, what skills you must master and the quality of relationships you build.

Not only is imagining a vivid future good for you and those around you, it is also good business.

Thinking about the future and making decisions to guide your actions from a future perspective is more exciting than thinking about your past or believing you will be stuck with your present circumstances forever. If you want to double or triple your organization's revenue in the next three years, then begin to think now how to create this future vision. This will help you decide what things you will say yes to and what things you will pass up. The concept is the same if you are leading a $5 Million organization and you want your future organization to be $15 Million. You can begin to create this reality now.

Be intentional!

You do realize, I hope, the actions and steps you've taken to be where you are today are beneficial because this is the same process you will need to grow your own future. However, by being intentional, you will be sharper, more focused and get the results you want quicker. Your quickest path to creating your future is to vividly imagine what you want your future to be. When you develop a future vision, your commitments and actions are the road map of how you will arrive at your destination. A future perspective begins by asking the following questions and creating ideas you'll desire to realize.

Develop relationships!

Who will you need to build relationships with in the future? Who will you create relationships with now to help get you to where you want to be? Who do you want to invite on this journey?

Build revenue!

Where will this additional revenue come from? What clues gleaned from pondering the future tell you where your organization will serve next? What areas do you want to serve in?

Receive a paycheck.

This may surprise you, but unless you land a multi-year grant, what you think now about funding will certainly change. For many years I was in foster care and related services. During my tenure, funding changed dramatically for this area. Opportunities changed and obstacles are often very different than what I could have imagined several years ago. Everything about how we did things even three years ago is radically different.

Develop a plan.

Do you want your organization to have a different focus? What is your strategy and plan? How will you serve the people? How will you motivate your team and board of directors to join you on this journey? We'll discuss strategy later on in this book.

Be flexible.

You will have to pivot at times and make the best decisions you can with the information you have on hand. However, you need to develop a vision of your future. Identify what you want for your life.

You will grow as a leader as you learn to adapt to every turn and twist in your leadership life. Understand this, developing systems based on excellence and best standards will help you stay ahead of your competitors.

Continually innovate!

Look at what you can build on. Change or improve to create an organization and life so each is better able to provide a future even more rich and rewarding through constant innovation.

Consider hiring the best executive coach you can find. Not the most available coach, the best coach! My personal coach and mentor, Henry Whitlow, graduated from Harvard with a master's degree in Business Administration (MBA). He is currently teaching at a college in Atlanta. He is a professor, a military veteran and familiar with industry at all levels. He was a soldier about the same time I was in military service. My coach can be trusted and I know he is always looking out for my best interests even though he and I are very different. He is black and I am white. However, when we talk, our discussions lead to exponential growth!

Select a Coach.

Start by testing your candidate:

A couple test questions I use for choosing a coach are:

- Do they continue following your eyes with theirs when you are talking?
- Do they value what you say?
- Do they add value to your life?
- Are you enlightened by their responses and feedback?
- Can they teach you something you don't know?

Be Curious

The cornerstone of being a great leader is curiosity! One of the hallmarks of great leadership is to wonder why something is the way it is and then ask questions. When you have answers, then ask more questions. If you make more statements than ask questions, you are wasting everyone's time including your own.

Respect people

Don't bore them with stories about yourself.

Incentivize

Incentivize your leadership to grow at a healthy rate with the mindset of ownership for your leaders.

An Exercise:

Take 10 minutes and write out where you want to see your organization in three years. This description could include the size of your agency or the activities you will be involved in as well as whose lives you will be impacting. If you want, think about how much revenue your organization will be bringing in each year.

Now, do the same for yourself. What does your future self-look like three years from now? What will you be doing? What problems will you be solving? Who will you be doing life with in three years?

DEVELOP A PHILOSOPHY
FOR LIFE AND LEADERSHIP

"The essence of strategy is choosing what not to do."

Michael Porter

Leadership has everything to do with how you see your world. It is about your mindset, perspectives, attitude and the principles you live by. Your world is influenced by these four things. It is wise to develop this philosophy for your work and life. A single philosophy can serve both. Without a philosophy or framework of the world you're in, you may experience chaos in your thinking.

My personal philosophy and leadership philosophy complement and support each other. From my experience, whenever I lack a clear view of the world, I become a follower, not a leader.

Without a developed philosophy, we all suffer from disorientation and possibly even a distortion in our thinking.

The privilege of leadership comes with a cost. Usually the cost is peace of mind. If you don't have a philosophy and, hopefully, a theology, you will have many miserable moments as a leader. Having a life philosophy has done more for my mental health and ability to make decisions without self-doubt and anxiety. My philosophy is very consistent with Stoicism. To me, Stoicism is the ability to make decisions without being wrapped up in emotions. The more rational I am when making decisions, the better off I am. It doesn't mean I am devoid of emotions. I simply try not to have them kick my butt!

I pay attention to my emotions and use my intuition. However, these are not the overriding things I pay attention to. I do not want to be ruled by emotion.

You may already have a theology or spiritual life and this will help you do the work of creating a whole life philosophy.

"Your philosophy determines whether you will go
for the disciplines or continue the errors."

Jim Rohn

In the previous chapter we talked about designing your next three years! In setting out on this course, you will need to have values and principles in which you can believe.

Stephen Covey, author of *The 7 Habits of Highly Effective People*, emphasizes the importance of aligning personal goals with one's core values to ensure a coherent and fulfilling life.

According to Covey, when our goals are in harmony with our values, we live and work with greater integrity and effectiveness. Here is how Covey suggests aligning core values with goals:

When you design your future, it is important to ask yourself, what are my core values. These would be core values for your organization including fundamental beliefs and principles used to guide your behavior and decision-making. You can tell if you have a great leadership philosophy by how well you turn ordinary people into extraordinary. Your legacy will be determined on how you turned a person with potential into an exceptional leader. Getting superior results from average people is the sign of a leader who knows why and how they do what they do!

Steven Covey is one of the most important literary mentors I ever encountered. My core values come out of my experience studying Covey's approach. Much of Covey's work was patterned after Peter Drucker, the father of modern management. I greatly respect both men for their respective achievements and insights.

Live your life by values

Continuing to see growth in others as they gain more capability in their life is important to me. A question I continually ask myself when I am leading others is whether the lives of those I'm leading are being changed.

Value innovation

I believe an organization needs to continually find more ways to serve people. I want to be a person who is instrumental in presenting new and better ways of providing services. If you are a brilliant innovator, the rest of the crowd will show up at the place you've just vacated and moved on from!

Who enjoys competition? I don't. However, I do like to be the best I can be and lead an organization to present the best services possible. I'd rather be a creator than a competitor.

As much as possible, I recommend you should only deal with people and organizations who are interested in you and your success! This is not always possible. However, it is a value to examine when starting a new professional relationship or continuing in a relationship with the people and organization where you are currently.

Position your organization where the funding is best in the areas you are interested in providing services. Over the long run, you want to be in areas where you are funded well and respected by the funder, as well as able to influence and be influenced by the people with whom you work.

Another important value is to influence others even as you allow them to influence you through mutual interactions.

Begin with an end in mind

This is a value I use daily and sometimes hourly. I try to identify how I want things to turn out before I enter a meeting, sign a contract or hire a new employee. Working backwards from the desired end goal helps me deal with constraints and focus my aim on what I want for our organization.

These are some precepts I prefer:

- Treat with dignity the people for whom I serve and work.
- Look out for the best interests of the people I serve.
- See others with the perspective of caring for and about them.
- Live from a loving mindset!
- Live with integrity and honesty.

Over all, I believe life should be lived by principles. Principles need to guide my leadership. Leading my family and parenting my children also require principles. If I achieve external goals in ways contrary to my values, I will pay for them in shame and guilt. It will also harden my soul. I will also know this is a low point in my life I will possibly be reminded of for a long time, perhaps to the end of my life.

Others are watching me as a leader in my community and organization. Therefore, my character should remain beyond reproach. Principles should be integrated into your daily life! They need to be a part of you! It is important to always look at the decisions you make and ask yourself what value or principle are you acting on.

Asking myself this question keeps my decisions in alignment with my values and principles and allows others to see very clearly my leadership philosophy! This will include decisions, reactions as well as what goals to pursue and why. The more we match what we do with our values and principles, the more the world will take notice. Acting this way ensures your path to achieving your goals even as it strengthens your character, integrity and reputation!

Outstanding leaders and motivators of our time use the following ways to design and accomplish their goals.

Visualize the results

Begin with the end in mind. This is a key tenet from Steven Covey's philosophy and leadership style. Imagine what you want, then ask yourself what steps you must take to achieve what you want. This step is worth your effort! Do it! You'll soon begin to achieve clarity with each new step you take.

As I wrote this book, my organization was preparing for the future. In the last three years, every aspect of our work changed. Programs, services and funding we relied on for years decreased by more than 40 percent. Many of my peers in other agencies left the field I continued to work in.

Concurrently, I am managing the future I designed and am planning for a new future. This is a constant process, designing our future and living in this future and then continuing in the process of designing the future for yourself and your organization.

Lead by principles

For leaders, this can be defined as a consistent and ethical approach to leadership where decisions and actions are clearly guided by a defined set of core values and beliefs.

> *"Management is doing things right;*
> *leadership is doing the right things."*

Peter Drucker

Here's a breakdown of what this entails:

Leaders use principles to act as an internal compass, thereby directing the leader's behavior even in challenging situations. By clearly communicating their principles, leaders empower others to make decisions in alignment with the organization's values. This fosters autonomy and accountability. When leaders consistently adhere to their principles, they create a culture of integrity and trust. This strengthens the organization and attracts individuals who share these values.

In essence, leading by principles is about:

- Being authentic.
- Acting with integrity.
- Creating a culture of trust.

It's about more than just achieving results. It is about how those results are achieved.

Recently while attending a conference, I noted three different speakers quoted the same author, a leader in organizational management, and shared the same quote.

"If you don't have margin,
you don't have a mission."

Peter Drucker

This principle or core belief is a cornerstone in each of the nonprofit organizations I led. It influences my perspective of finances, what services we offer and how we spend our money. For me, it is basic to surviving and thriving!

A principle is a normal or natural part of what you do. It must be clear. My principles guide me through the swamps and chaos of life. My peace of mind comes from relying on my spiritual beliefs and life philosophy.

Another principle I use is to make any final decisions only after talking with as many people as I can find who might be affected by the decision. In any situation, I want to know how I view the issue philosophically and what principles I am acting on. This helps in situations when someone else questions or challenges my reasoning. It also helps in stressful situations where my character may be questioned.

I gradually came to grips with one of the biggest issues: Am I supposed to be sacrificing everything to accomplish the mission of the organization or am I supposed to also run this organization like a business.

Principles make relationships easier to maneuver. I recall mentoring a junior leader. She was upset with another leader in our organization. The former was telling me of her dissatisfaction with the other leader's decisions and his attitude towards her.

This prompted me to recall another principle from Steven Covey's work. My suggestion to her was, "Seek first to understand, then be understood."

Everyone has his or her own perceptions and it would be valuable to find out what the other person's perception are before mismatched perceptions make things worse, I explained. Eventually, they did talk things out and discovered there were indeed errors in each of their ways of perceiving a certain situation. Once each person realized this, they were able to resolve their differences.

As I talked with the other leader, we both realized the other person was angry, yet he made no effort to understand why. This resulted in the decisions they each were making. This principle of understanding each other works whenever relationships go awry. Each leader has since put this tool or paradigm into his or her mental toolbox for future use.

One saying sticks with me: *"Make the hard easy!"*

I don't recall where the phrase originated, however, I heard it early in my career and it was foundational in everything I did thereafter from creating systems to designing programs. Making the hard easy guides me in creating incentives for my employees. Seeing the hard as easy paves the way to solutions where complexity needs to transform into simplicity, thus propelling you swiftly to the truth and a way forward!

> *"Complexity is your enemy.*
> *Any fool can make something complicated.*
> *It is hard to make something simple."*

Richard Branson

A partner concept is: *Simple is fast!*

"Simplicity is the ultimate sophistication."

Leonardo da Vinci

This doesn't mean finding a solution will be easy. Usually, it requires a lot more brain calories to make a process simple. Making the hard easy is more than a cute statement to me. It is a way of looking at life. From getting in shape to creating a marketing plan. In my experience, if it is not simple and easy to implement and measure, it won't last in either your organization or your life.

DESIGN YOUR OWN FUTURE

"The best way to predict the future is to create it."

Peter Drucker

Are you a nonprofit leader feeling the weight of uncertainty? Do you experience a nagging feeling the ground beneath your feet might suddenly shift at any moment? The stark reality is many leaders get trapped in the present and it's only a matter of time before their failure to continually redesign their future leads them directly into a crisis. Don't let stagnation be your story. Proactively redesign your tomorrows or someone else will rewrite the future for you.

Even the most forward-thinking individuals can be blindsided by ambiguity. Personally, I've navigated my share of uncertainty. This usually brings on a discomfort, at times, leading to painful delays. While those around me might see innovation and focus, I know from experience settling for the status quo is usually a recipe for eventual irrelevance. Truly exceptional leaders don't simply react to the future; they relentlessly shape it.

How do you conquer a fog of uncertainty which can paralyze progress? My proactive strategy is to seek out experienced guides or consultants who possess a bird's-eye view of the evolving landscape in my fields and the new territories my organization aims to conquer. By investing in this external expertise, you equip yourself and your team to not just adapt to change, but gives you the will to lead others to it.

Consider this: The very programs forming the bedrock of your organization for past decades might become obsolete within a mere five years. This shouldn't be a cause for despair.

Rather, let it be a powerful catalyst for innovation. The future holds a wealth of new opportunities, novel approaches to serving your mission and making an even greater impact. Embrace this inevitable evolution and you'll not only survive, but thrive.

This isn't mere theoretical advice. I actively live this principle. My approach involves visualizing the future of my agency — its potential size, the evolving suite of services — even if the initial map is just a rough sketch. The crucial point is to have an initial vision, a directional beacon to guide your steps. The finer details will emerge as you boldly move forward. Start with the big picture and the specifics will crystallize as you take decisive action.

Are you ready to elevate your organization to unprecedented heights?

The foundational process of setting clear goals and crafting a robust strategy is the very engine needed to propel you to the next level, granting you a clearer vision of what lies ahead. Remember the wisdom of a great strategist:

> *"Having a strategy matters,*
> *but what really matters is strategic thinking."*

Roger Martin

Cultivate this deep, analytical approach and you'll move beyond mere planning to true foresight.

What are the non-negotiable principles to anchor your organization's journey forward? Clearly articulate your core values and paint a vivid picture of where you intend to lead your organization. However, a word of caution. Avoid presenting an overly optimistic and potentially unrealistic picture to your board. Instead, invite them into your strategic thinking process by explaining the why behind each of your conclusions and allow them to contribute their own or collective valuable insights. This fosters a shared understanding of opportunities and helps clear inevitable hurdles along the pathway to your vision. Transparency builds trust and trust is the bedrock of unwavering support from your board of directors.

By openly sharing your strategic reasoning, you transform your board from a potentially critical audience into a unified and supportive team. Embrace their collective wisdom and you'll navigate future challenges with greater resilience and shared commitment.

Can you predict every twist and turn the future might throw into your pathway? Of course not! Setbacks, failures, and frustrations are inherent parts of any ambitious endeavor. However, by proactively involving your board in understanding inherent risks, you cultivate an environment where they are more likely to stand by you, provide sustained support and rally behind your efforts, especially when those inevitable storms arrive. Prepare your board for the journey and they will be your most steadfast allies.

What untapped powers do you possess as a leader? It's a remarkable ability to see the bigger picture. The ability to operate not just in the present but also with a clear understanding of the future you are collectively striving to create. When your actions are guided by this future-oriented perspective, you ignite a powerful culture of hope within the organization. Visionary leadership breeds unwavering belief.

> *"Your future is created by what you do today,*
> *not tomorrow."*
>
> **Robert Kayosaki**

Are you truly listening to the subtle signals illuminating the path ahead? It is absolutely crucial for you to pay close attention to any clues offered by your colleagues, consultants and coaches regarding the future landscape. These insights, often seemingly small or insignificant, may hold profound implications for your organization's future trajectory.

A seemingly minor anecdote from a staff member can be a critical early warning sign. Perhaps one person shares a story about a client's dissatisfaction or, conversely, a moment where your team made a significant positive impact. These seemingly casual remarks are invaluable data points about the evolving needs and perceptions of those you serve.

I vividly recall a pivotal moment sparked by a brief hallway conversation with Janice, one of our leaders. We were experiencing a decline in foster parents. This was a trend I was aware of but hadn't fully grasped the severity of until Janice's simple statement.

"We don't have enough parents to provide respite for our homes with children," Janice said.

Her words hit me with the force of revelation.

This single exchange, which took less than 30-seconds, was a catalyst for truly transformative action. It ignited a passion within me to streamline the process of creating new foster homes. Eventually, this became our agency's top priority. This singular clue propelled me on a mission to develop a comprehensive recruiting program which I then shared by teaching it to numerous agencies across the United States and Canada. Listening intently to one piece of information didn't just reshape our agency; it created a ripple effect which benefits countless other foster agencies to this moment.

This experience also propelled me onto the national stage as a speaker and recognized expert in foster parent recruitment. The lesson is clear: actively listen to what you are being told, then relentlessly ask yourself, "What does this mean for me, my people and our shared purpose?"

The results are often game-changing.

Early in my career, I observed another powerful clue by looking at the strategies and operations of agencies significantly larger than ours — generally, those operating at a scale of 3 to 20 times our capacity. Instead of succumbing to envy, I adopted a mindset of curiosity and analysis. I would meticulously examine their approaches, actively engage with their leaders and strategically evolve our own practices. My key question became, "Should we be implementing something similar in our organization?"

This exercise of proactive learning and adaptation led to the creation of five distinct divisions within our agency which, in turn, expanded our reach from a single service to a comprehensive portfolio of services encompassing education, mental health, transitional housing, services for homeless youth and philanthropy. Look beyond your immediate horizon and learn from those who have already charted the course you aspire to follow.

Executive Coaching

Are you investing in the most powerful tool for accelerating your leadership growth? In designing your life and leadership, engaging an Executive Coach is an invaluable investment. Commit to a minimum of six months with the very best coach you can find. The impact can be exponential.

As the saying goes:

"If I have seen further, it is by standing on the shoulders of giants."

Sir Isaac Newton

Never underestimate the transformative power of personalized guidance. My own organization experienced six-fold growth since I first embraced executive coaching. Even now, I continue to benefit from this powerful partnership. Continuous growth demands continuous learning and external perspective.

The specific reasons for needing a coach are unique to each leader. If your goal is to become a more effective leader, seek out a coach with a proven track record in leadership development. Importantly, your coach should possess the courage and insight to challenge your thinking, especially when a different perspective could lead your organization to better outcomes.

Great coaches don't just support you, they elevate your thinking.

Solve Problems by Streamlining Decision-Making

Are you making problem-solving a complex and time-consuming ordeal?

It doesn't need to be!

I rely on a straightforward process by developing a series of key questions and reminders to ensure thorough consideration. These steps have become so ingrained in my planning they are now almost automatic. By simplifying your own approach, I'll bet you will unlock clarity and accelerate your organization's problem-solving process.

My process involves asking myself:

- What is the core problem we are facing?
- What are the key variables at play? This includes identifying the individuals involved, the specific challenges we might face and each available option.
- What are the differing needs and desires of the various stakeholders?
- What actions should I take?
- What specific outcome would definitively resolve this issue?
- Will this resolution be satisfactory for all parties involved?
- Who might not have their needs fully met by this resolution?
- What proactive steps do I need to take in order to address this matter?
- How will I most effectively communicate these steps with others?

- Who are the essential individuals who need to be informed about this situation and the proposed solution?
- From whom do I need to gather additional information to make the most informed decision?
- What immediate decisions can I make with the information I currently have?
- What further information will provide the necessary clarity to confidently move forward?
- What are the potential unintended consequences of this situation and my proposed actions?
- Who else might be affected by my decision?

What is the right thing to do? This question requires courage. It is the ultimate question I always ask myself because at the end of the day, my actions must align with my values and I am accountable to all those who trust and support me. This guiding principle ensures integrity in every decision. It also helps bring clarity to those you help lead your organization.

This comprehensive checklist might seem exhausting. However, failure to consider these critical elements can lead to flawed decisions requiring significant time and effort to rectify these matters later. As the saying goes, the ability to simplify means to eliminate the unnecessary so the necessary may speak. Embrace this philosophy and you'll cut through the noise to the heart of any matter. Remember this truth from an American jazz composer, pianist, bassist and author:

"Making the simple complicated is commonplace.
Making the complicated simple, awesomely simple, that's creativity!"

Charles Mingus Jr.

ACTION STEPS FOR DESIGNING YOUR NONPROFIT'S FUTURE

1. **Schedule a Future Design session:** Dedicate at least one half-day each month to proactively envision the future of your organization. Ask what trends are emerging? What new needs will your community have? What innovative services can we develop?

2. **Identify and engage Future Guides:** Seek out consultants, advisors or thought leaders in your field and related sectors. Schedule regular check-ins to gain insights into emerging trends and potential disruptions. (Note: Your understanding of this concept will become clearer in a later chapter when I describe how a consultant's suggestion was ultimately worth $3 Million annually to one of our divisions.)

3. **Conduct a Clue Audit:** Implement a system for actively soliciting and documenting feedback and observations from staff, clients and stakeholders. Regularly review these clues for emerging patterns and potential opportunities or threats.

4. **Establish a Learning from Leaders Protocol:** Identify three to five organizations significantly larger or more innovative than yours. Research their strategies and reach out to their leaders for informational interviews. Identify at least one key practice you can adapt or experiment with in your own organization.

5. **Invest in Executive Coaching:** If you don't already have one, commit to finding and engaging an executive coach for at least a six-month period. Define clear goals for your coaching engagement and actively work with your coach to achieve them.

6. **Implement a Problem-Solving Protocol:** Adopt and consistently use the problem-solving framework outlined earlier to ensure thorough and ethical decision-making in all critical situations.

7. **Facilitate a Board Visioning Workshop:** Engage your board of directors in a dedicated session focused on collaboratively envisioning the organization's future. Encourage open dialogue, address potential challenges and build a shared understanding of the strategic direction.

8. **Create a Service Innovation Pipeline:** Dedicate resources to exploring and developing new programs and services to align with your future vision. Encourage staff to contribute ideas and create a structured process for evaluating and piloting innovative initiatives.

9. **Regularly Articulate Your Vision:** Consistently communicate your future-oriented vision to staff, board members, donors and the wider community. Paint a compelling picture of the impact you aim to create in the years to come.

10. **Embrace Strategic Thinking:** Go beyond simply creating a strategic plan. Cultivate a mindset of continuous questioning, analysis and adaptation. Make strategic thinking a core competency within your leadership team.

By implementing each of these action steps and embracing a future-focused mindset, you, as a nonprofit leader, can move from navigating uncertainty to confidently designing a thriving and impactful future for your organization.

LEAD FOR RESULTS!

To become a great leader requires a change in your lifestyle in order to obtain the results you want. As with any worthwhile endeavor, great leadership requires private work to achieve desired results. The work you do in private, however, will soon become evident to the public.

In my experience, it takes hours of reading, workshops and discussions with more advanced leaders to really learn the nuances of leadership. There are, perhaps, natural leaders. However, most of the masterful leaders I meet worked hard to achieve their status.

Leaders embrace the idea of innovation at some point in their career. The earlier the better, I say. Innovative leaders know change will inevitably come whether in the form of external changes forced on the organization or internal changes in thinking the leader has embraced. Each of these will affect how the leader directs the organization as it reacts to change.

"Innovation distinguishes between a leader and a follower."

Steve Jobs
Co-founder, Apple Inc.

Leaders who do what is necessary and right for themselves usually must overcome the fear in others less accustomed to change. The greatest leaders do what they fear themselves. Sometimes this causes leaders to take actions which place themselves in positions they've never been in before. One thing is assured, when you do a challenging thing, it changes you. You develop the skill and courage to take on the next challenge. The cool thing about this, it isn't as high a reach from the last perch you stood on to accomplish your next goal.

My jobs after military service were as a factory worker, a miner and working on the Rio Grande railroad in Colorado. Each career change required more from me. When I left the blue-collar world to go into straight commission sales, I faced fears and learned skills which helped me throughout the rest of my life.

*"You gain strength, courage and confidence by every
experience in which you really stop to look fear in the face.
You must do the thing you think you cannot do."*

Eleanor Roosevelt

The 80 Percent Rule!

I have seen many different types of leaders. Some leaders keep as much information to themselves as they can. Other leaders share everything so everyone they work with will know the why of each situation. I insist leaders who work for me share their job duties with their subordinates. Loosely, I have always believed whenever a key person leaves our organization, either by death or an immediate reason, we will be okay if we've done this one thing. We need to be able to pull together 80 percent of the vacant position's skill set in order to retain the level of excellence we prefer to maintain in our program. This 80 percent skill set is usually available from those who know the leader's job or were aware of what the leader did on a daily basis.

As a leader, I need to know whether we can replicate a person's job performance to the level of 80 percent of their knowledge. The remaining 20 percent can come from me as a leader, or the organization can replicate or replace the missing knowledge from another source.

This one action will save you dollars, time and stress if you ever lose a key employee. However, key employees aren't always an executive. Quite often, key employees might be an important clerical person whom everyone relies on!

Curiosity is the litmus test of a true leader!

You won't be a true leader until you've developed another leader to take your place or replace someone else's position of leadership. This pertains especially to the leaders who might leave your organization while either running an entire organization or one of its divisions.

Creating capable leaders is the fruit of a good leader.

*"I start with the premise that the function of leadership
is to produce more leaders, not more followers."*

Ralph Nader

My friend and executive coach Henry Whitlow taught me a lesson when he reinforced the concept I hold dear about asking questions being more important than coming up with answers!

"Curiosity is the core of leadership."

Henry Whitlow

It is my belief this is the one thing which truly makes a leader great! **Be Curious!**

Never see a person as ordinary. Know their struggles, their gifts, why they may have experienced difficulties at their previous job yet are excelling with you and your organization. Ask them how they achieved journeyman electrician status and how they feel about their accomplishments.

If you're not curious about those around you; what are you curious about? Do you know how your son is feeling about not getting an invite to the seventh grade basketball team? Do you ask questions, or are you more inclined to make statements? Questions change people. Statements close conversations or minds and end wonderment.

"A leader is best when people barely know they exist.
When his work is done, his aim fulfilled,
they will say: We did it ourselves."

Lao Tzu

When you ask questions, especially when you ask others about their perspective or when you ask others what they think about a particular problem your organization is facing, you will find most of the answers will actually come from others.

It is not necessary or wise to take the credit when you are teaching others to think. You have brought about the answer because you want more and better perspectives of all aspects of your organization. Know and appreciate your leaders for their great answers!

Succession

After 25 years leading a dynamic organization, I left my agency to begin the next phase of my life. Judging my leadership as well as yours should be based on how many leaders you created during your tenure of leadership and how well the organization is flourishing once you depart.

How often have we seen a great leader drive an organization to become better and grow larger only to learn, once they are no longer in the picture, the organization begins to lose its edge. Maybe the organization begins to lose vitality. The organization might still continue to exist for a time, yet its vitality is gone.

It is important to create other leaders within your organization. When I consult with an agency, I like to determine how deep is their leadership pool? Who will step into leadership when needed? As I mentioned earlier, you should be able to put together 80 percent of the knowledge needed if a division leader or a top clerical person leaves you. There are all kinds of tests you can do and a lot of information you can access to see where you are with the succession of your agency.

A very simple test for this is to ask yourself: Who will replace me? What skills and knowledge are needed by the next person to succeed me? How can I help the person who will replace me?

This question is a good one for every position in your organization! Don't wait. At my 25th year of leading the organization, I asked this question of those in attendance at our Christmas party. Who has 18 years or more of service within our organization? Since I founded the organization, I hired, fired or saw many people leave our organization. However, learning I still had three people with more than 18 years of service working with me gave me great satisfaction.

The point is this. Very few people will stay with you during a long tenure at the top leadership position. Therefore, you must prepare for people leaving. You will do yourself great service by doing so.

The better our depth of leadership, the better we can handle situations when top people leave, transfer or are promoted. If we have a good second person trained for each position, our leadership is almost seamless when it comes to producing or solving problems.

I firmly believe leaders are not born. They are made.

However, you can develop leaders. One of the best ways to do this is to give the lower level of leadership assignments to promising individuals, then observe the gifts they already possess, while helping them develop their best capabilities.

One of my greatest experiences was having my personal assistant grow in her position. Before she came to us, she worked at a large fitness gym. Her resume really didn't begin to show all of her capabilities. As we observed her doing little things in our company, we soon realized she was adept at doing everything quickly, caring about the results we wanted and executing these tasks in a timely fashion.

At one point, I asked my personal assistant to select a consultant so we could gain our national certification for the next three years. We held sufficient trust in her abilities to accomplish this critical project.

Her assignment was to review several consultants who were professionals in the field and give us her opinion of the top three candidates. She completed the task and two weeks later presented us with the names of the top three consultants.

Before scheduling any interviews, she gently suggested, "I think you'll like the folks from Boston best."

She was right. The consultants she believed would serve us best were thorough and absolutely on their game.

When you give people responsibilities they have never done before, it can be risky. However, it will soon show you the level of their competencies as well as the range of their capabilities.

Knowing someone's capabilities greatly assists the organization in succession planning.

There is more to leadership of a nonprofit than compassion!

Sad to say, many nonprofit leaders think compassion and empathy are the only two permissible traits a leader should have. While it's true empathy and compassion are some core traits of a leader, they do not comprise all the traits a leader needs.

A leader needs to be more than a cheer leader, consoler or therapist!

They also need to be a visionary, a guide who has clarity about the future. A leader needs to be a straight communicator who can put across a point and present a message to guide others. True leaders also should be able to influence others while also willing to be influenced by the knowledge imparted by others. They need to be good at communicating, yet also understand the most important part of communication is listening.

They need to exhibit kindness and consideration while accomplishing or exceeding the organization's goals. They need to be compassionate when needed and firm when required. They need to lead, yet also understand they need followers to comprehend where the organization is heading.

How to build capacity in those you lead

Assign your people to complete small tasks or take responsibility for smaller parts of the organization such as a department or division. Coach them during the completion of these smaller tasks. This will produce your future leaders and create a bond between you. Also, take time with existing leaders to listen to what issues they are encountering. Have them tell you how they are proceeding with problems they are confronting.

CREATE A THINKING TEAM

Getting results is a leader's responsibility. Mobilizing the energy of others and working towards a common goal should be a leader's focus. A leader's legacy will include personal actions as well as the results of those actions. This concept is nothing new, yet it remains relevant and important to understand.

I attended a conference some years ago and shared breakfast with a friend who knew many attendees who previously worked for him and were now leading their own agencies. He continued to enjoy a great relationship with those past employees. During the course of our meal, a steady stream of his former employees stopped by our table to say hello.

I found this ritual both amusing and revealing.

When each person left our table side, my friend would say the same thing.

"He (or she) sure knows how to get things done!"

We all admire people who get things done. What leaders must be clear on is to divide our time between moving our agency forward into the future and managing the problems brought to us daily.

In my past work with drug and alcohol treatment programs, the intensity and drama was often quite absorbing. If leaders become too consumed by the problems surrounding them, they often forget about their position of leadership. It's fine to help out and do tasks you are gifted to do from past experience. However, a leader's primary responsibility is to take on those things only you can do. Leave the rest to others whom you have trained to complete those tasks.

Because of your leadership position, you will be brought untold numbers of problems. When this happens, it is time to ask yourself this question.

Why is this problem being brought to me? How should I respond in this situation.

Also ask yourself this: "Do I want my people to solve problems or do I want them to be solely dependent upon me?"

You might think this is a contradiction. On one hand, I'm saying your job is to get results. On the other hand, I am asking whether you are compelled to give an answer to every subordinate.

However, it's not always this simple.

First, as a leader, I need to give some thought to what is being asked of me and why. Is the problem something to be resolved at a lower level? If not, why not?

Secondly, have you developed the appropriate systems for your team to make decisions. Is there a clear process to determine the appropriate level when a problem requires a leader's attention?

My favorite question for people who come to me with a problem is to ask. "What are your thoughts on the matter?"

This question will reveal what the other person is already considering. It also may give a leader deeper understanding of what is the real or underlying issue creating the problem.

It is important to ask this question because it will help you determine when to provide feedback. If you give your opinion too soon, invariably, the person will respond, "I tried that already."

What's Your Plan?

My other favorite question is to ask, "What's your plan?"

I want people to learn how to think, to use their brain calories before they come to me. After you ask this question, don't say anything until they respond fully.

I want to grow the capacity for problem solving within my team. We can accomplish more and they will be more accomplished if we all own the problem and spend some time thinking about a workable solution.

My next question is usually, "Is there anything else?"

Once you have their response, then you have an opportunity to teach or coach. This is the appropriate time to teach them how to think through a problem more thoroughly and develop new paradigms or perspectives on solving problems for themselves.

If I have some items I believe they should pay attention to, I will say: "You've done a good job thinking this through, I especially like ______."

Or, if there is something they missed, I'll say: "I do have a nuance to suggest."

This is when I offer them suggestions on elements they missed while analyzing the problem. These suggestions are usually appreciated. Finally, I encourage my leaders to add these suggestions and their own solutions to their work plan.

It is also important to follow up by asking: "What do you think of the suggestions I just made?"

"Do you think they go well with your plan?"

I take these specific steps whenever a leader meets with me to resolve a problem:

1. Listen to a full description of the issues.

2. Ask for any additional information that could prove helpful.

3. Ask for their solution or plan.

4. If they seem confused, peel the onion back another layer by asking: "What solutions have you already thought about?"

5. Then ask: "What concerns you most about this situation?"

6. After following this format, suggest a few nuances they might want to consider. At such a point, provide your input. Surprisingly, almost everyone appreciates understanding the steps to their work process if it will solve difficult situations.

7. Next, follow up later to see whether the problem was solved. Do this as soon after the person successfully implements their plan of action.

One of my most trusted and capable division leaders came to my office one day with an issue. "We are going to have an adoption party for Robin, a 4-year-old girl," she said.

Robin was to be adopted along with an older sibling. However, her brother's behavior created challenges so serious he was unable to join his sister as part of her new family. The decision by all the professionals involved was to hold an adoption party for Robin. Later, staff hoped the older brother would also be adopted.

As I listened to this respected leader, she invited me to attend a party at the foster home currently housing the two children. After asking a few more questions, it grew apparent to me having an adoption party for just one child was not the best idea.

I enquired if I might offer some feedback and she agreed.

The older brother may misperceive the celebration of his younger sister's adoption and possibly act out against his sibling, I suggested. The boy might even begin to regress in his own behavior because he is not being adopted or celebrated, I added. Being a brilliant person, our leader quickly caught the error of her plan and changed it immediately.

"I get it. I hadn't thought of it that way. Thank you. Mike. This could have gone south on us and caused this young boy unneeded pain!" she said.

This points to the value of having others use their own brain, yet remaining flexible if a better solution presents itself.

- When leaders teach people to think through problems, both sides benefit. We develop more competent employees because they become accustomed to thinking at another level. This increases their value to the organization. As a result, they and the organization each increase in capacity, compassion and efficiency.

- The ability to think is better for everyone. They also grow as employees and people.

- When I teach employees to think for themselves, the employees and I go from a dependent relationship model to an inter-dependent relationship model where we each receive immense value.

I remember when Henry, my coach, asked me this same question. It came during a conversation with him when I shared a personnel issue. It involved a situation I was reluctant to solve. I had a long-term relationship with a leader who I thought was keeping our organization from growing. I showed anger and resentment towards the person because it appeared he was just interested in everything staying status quo.

When I shared with Henry my perspective, he responded with one of his Henry-isms.

"Too bad, Mike. Sounds like this really upsets you."

I knew there was more to come from Henry.

"What's your plan?" he eventually asked.

Although annoyed, I also understood Henry's question was based on his own perspective of responsibility. In other words, if I encountered a problem within the organization, I was supposed to step up and take responsibility for finding a solution to the problem.

It soon became clear to me I was the one who needed to change my attitude. Also, I needed to approach this problem with courage. Later, I confronted the person and within three months, the person found a position with another organization. The result of me taking the lead and developing a plan meant our organization could now move forward with more speed.

You can use this question when you are meeting with someone you supervise or even a peer. Begin the conversation by saying, "Welcome, John, what's going on with you?"

This may prompt John to describe a problem or dilemma he is dealing with so listen intently. When John stops talking, gently ask a few clarifying questions. Once you've heard enough to understand his dilemma, ask John: "What's your plan?"

Here's where the magic happens.

Sometimes John will look at you in an irritated way and say, "I don't know!" Quite possibly this response will be accompanied by a sarcastic tone implying "If I knew how to solve the problem, I wouldn't be talking with you."

My coach Henry Whitlow was the first person to use this question on me. He did so with extraordinary skill!

I quickly learned to use this question in almost every situation where someone brings my attention to an issue and wants me to solve it. For example, when one of my staff comes to me and tells me about a problem with resources or another person's attitude, whether it be a colleague, supervisor or someone they supervise, I use the powerful question: "What is your plan?"

Why is this question so important?

Well, it does several things:

It helps people learn how to think through problems on their own. As a leader you've likely realized most people don't know how to think through a problem even after successfully completing a college education and quite possibly an advanced degree. Some people would rather be told an answer than think of one on their own. They would rather force others to use brain calories instead of using their own.

Secondly, it is consistent with my value of not creating dependency. Embarrassingly, in my early years of leadership I tried to know everything and have all the answers. As I mentioned before, I love being in command. I was the center of everything and everything revolved around me. While this was great for my ego, it didn't help me create a better team and enable them to make decisions at the lowest possible level. Before I started using the "What is your plan?" approach, every problem came to me.

The third reason I want people to formulate their own plan of resolving issues is because of succession. I want my staff and leaders to completely understand the organization and how to function within it as efficiently as possible. Leaders don't stay around forever. Therefore, they need to see how other people process situations and solve problems.

There is another reason people in an organization need to think through issues and develop a plan of action or correction. One big reason involves growing your organization. Leaders quickly discover they can't be everywhere and do everything. Future leaders must develop a capacity to think and make decisions on their own. The more experience they have doing so, the more successful your organization becomes.

At a certain point in life, you may desire a different position within your agency or tackle a difficult situation in your personal life. For example, as our agency grew larger, I wanted to quit involving myself in day-to-day operations. Training my people to think for themselves by asking them "What is your plan?" allowed me to let go of many routine details so I could pay more attention to the organization's mission and vision.

Get your people to think!

The worst thing to happen after you ask, "What is your plan?" is for them to respond: "I don't know."

Don't pick up this bone. Your next response should be: "You're bright enough so I know you wouldn't come to me without having mulled this matter over. What have you already thought about?"

The benefit to this question is you don't immediately respond to them. This gives them another opportunity to think through some possible solutions.

The second advantage, you learn what they are considering and this will help you formulate a better response when it's appropriate. It also keeps you from wasting your own valuable time. You will also eliminate the formulation of an answer only to be told: "That won't work. I've already considered what you're suggesting."

The third benefit: Now you can provide meaningful advice by suggesting some nuances they may not have considered. This response should come only after they have thought through the problem on their own and responded appropriately with their best solution. Nuances help you to keep the person in line with your thinking and the organization's greatest need. They are also great tools to identify potential problems others missed or might surface once they have time to prepare a response.

Master these techniques and you can use them several times a day. Most people won't really recognize how you are getting them to think for themselves. They will also learn from you more knowledge than they have before as well as how to think deeply on subjects.

This is a powerful skill bound to make you a more effective leader.

Recently, I was coaching one of my executives on how to teach subordinates how to think. Now, this might sound insulting at first, so ask yourself this question: "How many people come to me with a problem which I end up solving without forcing them to use any of their own brain calories"?

If you are like me, you want to be accessible to those you supervise. It's great to develop rapport with people. However, most leaders don't want their time wasted. What I ask myself is this: "Do I value being important to people more than to develop people into becoming problem-solving free-thinking individuals?" It is important to lead by exposing new and old leaders to new perspectives or ask questions which force them to think deeper.

One unintended consequence of coaching someone is they begin to think in the ways you think. This might seem boastful or arrogant. However, I believe most leaders realize they are creating a culture. When the people I supervise ask themselves, "What would Mike think about this?" or "What would Mike do?" I realize they do this because they know and trust me, so out of honor and respect, their desire is to come up with the best answer.

*"A good leader takes people where they want to go.
A great leader takes people where they ought to go
but don't necessarily want to go, yet ought to be."*

Rosalynn Carter

Motivate people to treat the organization as their own

It is my goal to have employees feel as if they own the organization. This means they are doing for the organization and each other what they would do if the organization was their own or they were the founder. The following are some tactics to accomplish that goal:

When you want the best from your people, start out with a question as well as a direction.

For example, I want people who attend a meeting to get involved and have greater buy-in of the topic. I want them to grow accustomed to speaking publicly and sharing their own opinions. Therefore, I create a safe space by teaching them how to act in a group setting while still retaining the ability to voice their personal perspectives. Helping people get beyond their fear of public speaking and express themselves in an environment where their ideas are supported is what real leaders do. People who aren't used to speaking in a group can be very emotional or uneasy at articulating their thoughts.

Speak to those individuals before the meeting and tell them you want them to cover a very specific topic. By subtly adding this bit of direction, you will prevent them from losing the group's focus and thus believe they did a poor job.

Leaders quickly discover they need many things from others. For example, leaders benefit from soliciting different points of view and the hands-on knowledge they personally lack.

By encouraging workers to think through their own challenges and obtaining possible solutions from them, a leader can more quickly help the group develop answers to even the biggest problems.

It is important to obtain the workers' point of view. Many of them are likely thinking about problem solving as they go through various tasks, steps and processes of their daily duties. Encourage them to consider what direction the company should be taking in these areas. One topic on the visible horizon might include relocating offices, investing in another modality or creating a new industry. Sometimes it is to a leader's advantage to discover an opposing point of view prior to a meeting and help guide or mentor a presentation of the concept in order to lay out certain parts you intend to address.

Control the direction of a meeting:

There are other times where you may have to set up a more formal meeting structure.

For example, if you think a particular meeting will derail because a suggested outcome is counteractive, then begin the meeting with a statement such as this: "I want to hear all you have to say about this topic. Your opinion is important to all of us. Obviously, I will make the bottom-line decision on which way we move forward. However, I do need all of you to share your perspective."

Or:

"I'm going to guide the meeting so we uncover solutions for the specific areas needed. So please speak up and let's respect all ideas. We do want and need everyone's perspective."

When leaders do this, the following usually happens: You honor others by telling them their opinions are important! You express a need for them and value their input.

Help them realize they are an important part of your team. This will also reassure you when making the most appropriate bottom-line decision. My intention as a leader is to receive more perspectives than I originally held.

Almost always, this enables me to come up with an even better decision.

What also gets communicated to others is they are welcome to have their own perspective. However, at the end of the day, the leader does not give up his or her authority, even though others might hold strong opposing opinions.

As a leader, you do need authority. Authority doesn't mean using it in every instance. However, it does mean a leader knows how to access authority when needed.

Being authoritative should seldom be used in situations where you must say: "I am the boss!"

At times, however, saying this may well be necessary.

Seeking Guidance From a Mentor

I always look for guides!

At any time in the last 10 years, I have retained the services of at least three consultants. I like to call some of them my sherpas. You know, those guides who lead expeditions in Nepal when climbers want to scale Mt. Everest and stay alive in the process.

The value of these people is immeasurable! I was speaking with an educational consultant who I paid $5,000 for advice. At one of our meetings, I asked her whether we should apply for a specific grant. I was very doubtful it would be applicable to us and held a bias against applying because we likely would not be one of those agencies who received the award. I therefore asked, "Jen, do you think we should go to the effort of applying for the XYZ grant"?

She looked at me and replied, "Of course, this is right up your alley! I think you're the type of organization they want to give this grant to."

We did apply and my organization ended up receiving a grant worth $2.9 million.

For a $5,000 investment in advice, we received $2.9 million in operating funds. I would be happy to make this sort of trade all day long!

Having a guide's assistance through a specific issue or someone who is able to offer general guidance as an executive coach by acting as a trusted mentor is hugely important for a leader of any age or at any level of leadership!

It was always a goal of mine to seek out and hire the smartest, wisest and most knowledgeable people as guides, consultants or mentors and then learn whatever I could from them.

You would think finding such people is an easy task. However, my experience tells me either those people are very busy or sometimes they may feel inadequate or even threatened when I ask them to be a mentor. Perhaps it is because they don't feel perfect and don't want to be judged or disappoint me.

Fortunately, I was able on a few occasions to find exceptional people with whom I could build a true relationship. They are the ones who ultimately challenge me and guide me. The wisdom I receive in these relationships is so valuable. Their guidance is so powerful because, ultimately, I am then able to pass their insights along to the people I am mentoring or coaching.

Two of the finest people I know guided me through the hardest situations I ever encountered. One did so by asking me questions. The other allowed me to realize there were higher standards I needed to be looking at!

I love being mentored. One of the mentors in my life is my friend Pastor Jack Witt because of how differently we see things. His focus on understanding people as well as giving them grace helps me immeasurably!

My second mentor is Henry Whitlow, whom I mentioned earlier.

Both men make me think differently! For this, I am thankful.

Be influential, yet willing to be influenced!

Probably like you, I receive compliments about how wise or intelligent I am. Yet, I'd rather be a leader who asks the insightful questions or who, after hearing new information, is willing to adapt and be different. I want to be known as a leader who is willing to change his mind.

As leaders, it should be our goal to always be willing to change our minds when new information changes things! However, never change your mind to accommodate resistance or make people like you.

Years ago, I was involved in a situation where a professional in the community shared information through one of my leaders which I knew needed an immediate reaction. The professional apparently didn't like what he was hearing from my leader about my thoughts on a particular subject.

"I hear you want to handle this situation in a certain way," the professional confronted me.

I affirmed his assumption.

"I think you're wrong!" he replied.

"What do you think I am wrong about? What is your point of view?" I asked.

I listened to him, and he did make an interesting point or two.

"We have different points of view, but would you clarify what you saw as the weaknesses in my position," I responded when he was through speaking.

He gave me his perspective and I rethought my original position.

Then, I changed my mind and told him of my new plan.

"Well, you said you were going to take certain steps," the professional countered.

"Yes, I did. However, you provided new information and I needed to reconsider after what you told me."

He seemed surprised.

"What do you do when you get new information?" I responded.

He seemed amazed I could be so flexible and did not stubbornly hang on to my original conclusion.

We continued to converse. Eventually, an even more elegant solution became apparent to me. I then stated this third alternative course of action and he responded by calling me brilliant.

Ha! This always feels good!

We solved the problem we encountered and walked away respecting each other more than we did before. Therefore, a willingness to be influenced by others can make you more influential.

Two principles I use are: Seek to understand the other person's point of view. Then, be willing to change if new information brings you closer to the truth or a better solution. Being open to another point of view often leads to synergy and better ideas!

Values of great leaders!

As much as possible, I try to live my life based on values. When I do so, my decisions are better, I treat my people with more compassion and the outcomes are superior even to what I imagined them to be. Also, living by values allows me to face the outcomes of my decisions. I gain confidence because I know I made my decision based on the highest level of thinking available. The following values are what I use to do the right thing, come up with the best solutions and acquire the best information possible.

Values

Management by Wandering Around — sometimes shortened to the acronym MBWA – means the best way to manage is to get out of your office and go see what people are actually doing. Try to see what difficulties they encounter and build relationships as they grapple with the situation.

Don't wait for problems to come to you. Listen! Become a master listener. Many people will listen to your stories about your children or your problems. However, deep relationships are better built with the people you supervise when you listen to them tell their stories.

Some clues to being a better listener are simple, yet profound.

- Keep your eyes on them while they are speaking. If you break eye contact, you send a message something else is more important than your conversation.
- Ask open ended questions, especially those requiring an answer beyond a simple yes or no.
- Pay attention to answers and help them unpack what they are trying to say.
- Know how deep to go in each conversation. For new employees, you probably shouldn't ask the same questions you would ask a more seasoned employee.
- Keep your portion of the conversation to 30 percent.
- Pursue a problem or a new system until you know it was implemented or the problem solved. When starting a new system, make sure it is working. Follow up a few days after implementation, then again a month later or even after three months. Tweak the systems when necessary. Make sure the problem is solved and the solution sticks! Revisiting systems and solutions is imperative.

Do not show grace for any violation of standards and systems. Be firm. Fix it immediately. Make sure it doesn't happen again. Document the violation. If you have a conversation with an employee about a situation, document it. If you have a corrective action, remember to document it. A person who violates a standard needs to be monitored or the chance of it happening again will be heightened.

Don't unsolve what you have already solved!

One of the most important things you can do is to solve a problem and then don't unsolve it.

In my first leadership position after college, my staff and I were meeting with one of the lead nurses in our program to talk about their lack of professionalism, inconsistency in job performance and failure to meet company standards. The person was given a corrective action write up.

When the employee came into the room, I asked the person to sit as I described each of four infractions they committed before ending with my stern warning: "This will be the end of those behaviors."

It was a tense time, so I was straight to the point and firm.

What I experienced in the meeting was the person with the issues was very aware their job was in jeopardy if they didn't improve. It was also very clear I wanted a change in behavior and attitude. After the person responded and became emotional, he was finally willing to hear the changes we wanted him to make.

The next day, I followed up with the employee's supervisor and asked for her thoughts about the meeting.

The supervisor told me the employee actually came to her shortly after the meeting to ask whether he was written up. I listened to her explanation.

"Uh, not really. We just wanted to clarify some things for you. We really want to work with you," was the gist of the supervisor's response to the employee.

From her response, I realized she took the stance of least resistance and was trying to placate the employee with people pleasing. In reality, what she did was alleviate the corrected employee's personal responsibility for changing his behavior. Also, I was concerned the supervisor reduced the seriousness of any of the employee's infractions to the level of a pep talk.

I therefore directed the supervisor to recontact the employee and convey to him that she was in error. The purpose of my meeting with the employee was indeed to warn him of the corrective actions which would be taken if he did not change his ways.

What I noticed immediately was a universal problem in leadership. It happens with parents as well. It is the lack of being firm when someone receives corrective action. Parents want their children to love them so much they value appeasement over teaching the children principles and values. The lack of intervening in behaviors and holding clear lines of expected behavior are disappearing across our culture.

The unsolving of solved problems and the fixing of a problem and then not having the courage and conviction to be consistent with holding the line and firmly leading through change is ubiquitous.

Some leaders do not keep solved problems solved because of their own fears. They are fearful of telling the truth and being straight with a corrected employee. Leaders do not want to reemphasize what they expect of the employee.

My coach calls this "obstreperous behavior," meaning we are afraid the person will come back with an accusation, anger or create havoc within the organization.

After great thought and perhaps even getting counsel from others, leaders back away from positions they have announced because others don't like the resulting confrontation.

The Manager's Paradox!

A significant thing many new managers and some senior executives sometimes do is to seek the approval of those they are leading.

Being liked by people is fine. However, making decisions out of fear for another person's anger or dissatisfaction with a decision needs to be something all leaders should work to avoid.

Leaders are prone to hear a point of view from a certain group of people and then join a new group of people who want to discuss the same subject. The second group might hold a totally different point of view. This is where leaders often blow it. If they agree with the first group without hearing from the second or a third group, they leave themselves in a tight spot.

Why do I think they are in a tight spot? Well, if the leader talks to a second group and they see the problem clearer than the first group, the leader must then go back to the first group and tell them they do not have the best answer.

When a leader goes back to the first group, it is not just words he or she must communicate. The leader must deal with the first group possibly feeling deceived because they believed they are right. They might even challenge the leader by saying he or she agreed with them and now the leader is not backing them.

We would like to think the truth is what all people seek. However, we need to realize when people are upset, their dark side or whatever you want to call it, comes into play.

A leadership paradox is caused by one or more of these three elements:

- Lack of courage
- People pleasing
- Lack of skill

Lack of Courage

Lack of courage or the fear of people being obstreperous comes into play when a leader does something which must soon be undone or takes a course of action different from the norm which should be taken.

I met with one of my newest leaders and heard a story about another leader with whom she was collaborating in order to solve a certain problem. Both leaders agreed on a solution. However, one week later the other person came back and wanted to do something different than the course previously agreed upon.

The new leader asked me, "Why is she unsolving something we already solved?"

It turns out, all of this occurred because the other leader she was working with went back to the first group she made an agreement with, and this group was resistant to what she agreed upon with the other leader. The second leader chose not to push through the resistance. Instead, she gave in and reneged on her previous agreement with the first leader rather than suffer disappointment from her team by following through with the agreed upon solution.

The second leader also violated another of my principles which is to ask, "Who else do I want to get input from before I make a decision?"

People Pleasing

Being nice is sometimes a by-product of trying to be a compassionate person. More times than not, being nice often leads to people pleasing.

The genesis of these situations can almost always be found in wanting to please everyone and later getting caught up in a situation similar to the one I described above. In my opinion, people pleasing at its core is a lack of courage. Sometimes leaders in these situations are charismatic and very caring. If this is the case, people will soon develop a love/hate attitude towards these leaders. Eventually, the people they lead may want a different leader or even choose to leave the organization.

Lack of skill:

A powerful skill all leaders should develop is a desire to hear all sides of a situation. Sometimes it isn't obvious who all the stakeholders are in a complicated matter. However, it is the leader's responsibility to find out. The greatest value is to find and listen to a person who sees things from a completely different perspective or viewpoint. The best thing a leader can do is to hear everything valuable about a given situation in order to understand the situation in its entirety.

The first thing a leader shouldn't do is decide or take a side until he or she understands all perspectives. If certain people are pressuring the leader for a decision, he or she should develop the skill of saying something like: "I understand you want this solved, however, I need to talk to all involved so we can come up with the best solution that works for as many people as possible."

Creating win-win situations and seeking the best solutions or the truth should be the leader's ultimate goal. Once attained, this standard should be non-negotiable for any leader.

Idea Meritocracy

Idea meritocracy is the absolute gold standard for a leader. One who leads based on meritocracy wants to hear all points of view and then come up with the best answers. Meritocracy's basis is this: Ideas are judged and accepted based on merit, quality or effectiveness rather than on who proposed them. Idea Meritocracy values excellence and competence.

It takes strength to lead from this perspective. We all appreciate support and often jeopardize alliances when we choose ideas we were not loyal to in the past. However, a culture can be created with the value of meritocracy as a part of the decision-making process. Employees will soon change into people who want the best idea rather than champion only their own ideas.

Building a company which genuinely welcomes ideas from all employees is a challenge. However, in my experience, it has proved to continually lead us to a competitive position. Ultimately, it is rewarding and fulfilling to all who participate. If you haven't done this, it's one of the experiences you will never forget. It brings about an equality of thought. Eventually, you will find out which employees are thinkers. Those are the ones who are thinking through some of their problems or barriers and developing solutions you haven't yet thought of for your organization.

For example, we once needed to recruit more therapists when recruiting was our most challenging task. Our receptionist came up with the best idea. This one process provided us with the synergy we needed to move forward.

In the arena of meritocracy, the best ideas win. Generally, the person with the most information decides how the company will move forward. By putting the value of ideas at the forefront, you can cut through bureaucracy and ensure your organization is playing the best cards it holds.

This concept is often credited to Ray Dalio, the chief investment officer and co-chairman of Bridgewater, an investment management firm.

It's a radical idea for most business hierarchies to create a true idea meritocracy. Leadership must allow the person with the most thoughtful perspective based on the best information to make the decision, regardless of their tenure or rank.

Meritocracy works because:
- It helps you seize every growth opportunity.
- You cultivate a culture of active listening which ensures your employees feel confident in sharing their ideas.
- It democratizes your culture. Typically, the most insightful ideas come from those who engage with your products or services daily. However, these team members don't always hold the decision-making power and sometimes will hold back on expressing their ideas.

Employees who are deeply involved in day-to-day operations are well-placed to identify growth opportunities. They often have access to data which highlights the problems in need of solutions. They are also the ones dealing with barriers to implementation and most likely have suggestions for improving new systems as well as older systems in need of tweaking. Meritocracy supports your people in doing an excellent job!

Innovative ideas drive your company forward more quickly. The more freely employees share their ideas, the faster your organization will grow.

Implementing Meritocracy!

Here are some ideas to incorporate idea mediocrity in your organization.

Draw out employees who are usually quiet during meetings. One way to do this is to tell everyone you will ask each person for one or two ideas to make the organization better at some point during the meeting. This will give the people who tend to be introverts time to think and process their responses.

Maintain a perspective all ideas are welcome. Respect your employees' ideas. Let people know, whether in meetings or during private time, all points of view are welcome. Continually look for ideas to contribute from the janitor to the Chief Information Officer and anyone in between.

When your employees speak or offer suggestions, make sure your eyes are locked on them. By doing this, you grant value to what they say.

It may be annoying because sometimes their ideas will sound as if they are complaining. This is not unusual. People who previously did not have any voice in the organization will typically not be eloquent speakers. Therefore, their ideas will come in the form of a complaint. You can coach them later about how to better present suggestions. However, at first, be open to hear whatever they have to say.

Two things you should always keep in mind:

If you are concerned about an employee who is a center of influence making a statement with little or no proof which could create disruption in your meeting or organization, ask them prior to the meeting to submit data about the substance of their idea. Be proactive and ask them to demonstrate solutions for something they believe is or might become a significant problem.

When ideas are presented, have someone keep track of them. I once led a meeting for a division and started to write down on a whiteboard the various suggestions employees were making. By the time they were done, we had 24 ideas listed. After we prioritized them, we gave assignments to people in the meeting to follow up on each one. You'll want to hold a follow-up meeting so you and everyone else are held accountable for getting the desired results.

This is important: I believe leaders should be responsive to employees and, quite frankly, especially if we reach an agreement with them on a particular course of action. I also believe leaders should never put themselves in a position of groveling. After all, you hold ultimate responsibility once you take on the role of CEO or leader.

That being said, you can tell the group you desire to hear every idea. However, as CEO or leader, you will make the final decision as to whether an idea gets implemented and how it will be implemented. Idea meritocracy is one of the most powerful things you can do as a leader. If you are the smartest person in the room, it is time to get your team thinking and have them contribute at a higher level.

GUIDE THOSE YOU LEAD

The subject of managing results is often written about in books or magazines such as *Harvard Business Review* and is generally a popular topic for numerous **YouTube** videos or podcasts.

Most leaders take courses or attend conferences related to this subject.

In my 40th year of leading agencies in the social service realm, I thought it was time to address the dichotomy of leadership. I am referring now to the ways leaders motivate employees.

Granted, some employees need very little guidance. With a simple nudge, they are off to the races. Other employees, however, need oversight and monitoring to see a task to completion. This chapter will help you obtain favorable results with both types of people.

To me, this is the difference between intervention and nurturing. Other authors might call it the difference between compassion and results.

I am not devoid of compassion. Yet, when I lead, my focus is on obtaining results. However, more and more I am seeing our culture draw solid lines between getting results and being compassionate. Compassionate folks say the only way to get to results is through a culture of intense caring with a disregard for anything measurable and replicable. Those with another perspective believe results are the only way to measure the success of an organization. I believe you can do both. However, it takes more time and energy than choosing one route over the other.

I've worked in many types of environments and this issue always raises its head. This is especially true in social service agencies as well as in nonprofits.

A 2009 study by Jack Zenger and Joseph Folkman looks at how a leader's effectiveness is related to their ability to balance getting results with having good social skills. The study came up with some interesting statistics.

How common is the "Both" skillset?

They discovered approximately 13 percent of leaders were seen as equally strong in getting results and having good social skills. This shows it is rare to find leaders who excel at both skills.

How do skills affect perceived effectiveness?

The study broke down different skill combinations to show how they affect perceptions of a leader's effectiveness.

Results-focused but socially awkward

Leaders who are great at getting results but weak on social skills are only seen as effective at the 14th percentile. Think of it like this: if you lined up 100 leaders from least to most effective, these folks would be near the bottom.

Social butterflies but not results-driven

Leaders who are great with people yet not so focused on results did a little worse, but not much. They were at the 12th percentile in effectiveness. So, a little lower than the results-focused/socially awkward group and still not great.

Good at both

Leaders who are strong in both areas — results and social skills — are perceived way differently. They land in the 72nd percentile for effectiveness! This is a huge jump.

The Power of Balance

The study also shows how important it is to have a good balance of both skills. Leaders who are above the 75th percentile in both results and social skills are seen as exceptional. They are in the top 10 percent of all leaders when it comes to overall effectiveness!

These numbers really show how much difference it makes when a leader can balance being focused on results and maintaining strong social skills. While both sets of skills are valuable on their own, the study makes it clear the most effective leaders are the ones who can combine them successfully.

In response to this dilemma, I wrote a message to the six leaders in my organization.

"What is the best way to lead?"

My first position in human services was as director of a drug and alcohol unit at a hospital where I was indoctrinated into the art of intervention, a tool used to treat addiction and a tool we recommend to families of those addicted. However not everyone gets well and not everyone changes after an intervention.

As I progressed through my career, I was coached — although not willingly — to be more nurturing. Sometimes I realized how comforting the hurt and helping pick up the pieces of their lives was more powerful than telling them to get their act together or get out.

Nurturing doesn't always work either. People sometimes want to stay where they are and don't want to go down yet another path. To work with folks who aren't ready can be seen as a waste of time. It also uses up resources instead of finding some other client who would welcome the help.

This realization led me to the primary question: "How shall we lead?"

What is the best way?

My second question is this: "Am I leading for results or for relationships?"

In my position as CEO, I have typically led for results because this was what was expected of me. Doing this, however, was not as fulfilling as I would have preferred my work life to be. And it was not always effective.

However, leading for relationships does not always lead to results. I have also experienced organizations become gooey. By this I mean there are few standards, few accomplishments and a lack of dynamism. People like me usually don't stay long in those kinds of environments.

I trust you understand how this creates a dilemma.

I'd like to pass along a few bits of wisdom learned from my own experiences. At this advanced stage of my life and career, it's no longer presumptive for me to say I can see things a little more clearly. Therefore, I believe both perspectives — nurturing and intervention — are powerful!

A couple words of caution, however. Intervention works best when you must stop a situation before it leads to a person damaging themselves, another individual or an entire organization.

As leaders, we must know when it is most appropriate to step in and provide proper direction.

Nurturing works best when we help someone pick up the pieces, especially when their life requires it the most. This is usually when a person does not have the energy, direction or wherewithal to move in a positive direction.

Intervention requires compassion and firmness while nurturing works best with gentleness and structure.

Every person we lead needs guidance. Sometimes they need a lot, sometimes they need just a hint of direction. Remember, an employee without guidance is on their own. It is for this reason I love horse racing. Sometimes a jockey rides a horse in need of attention from the very first jump out of the gate. Sometimes blinders are put on a horse so they can only see forward. Sometimes other structures or encouragement are required to help them stay on track. At other times, there is little need for a jockey other than to provide a gentle nudge of a knee into the side of the horse or a slight movement of their hand on the reins. This is all the horse needs; a microscopic amount of guidance and a gentle cue is all they need to win the race.

It is my opinion everyone needs guidance on a regular basis.

This is where your leadership will shine. It is not easy and usually requires courage. As you practice, however, you will steadily become a more effective leader. All people need a person of courage who will say what is necessary when it needs saying.

In conclusion, the ones who need the most guidance will veer the farthest if they don't have attention paid to them on a regular basis. Without attending to this type of person, you may end up with yet another problem. It may only take a bit of direction or possibly there should be an intervention before the outcome will be deemed successful. Meanwhile, the ones who need little guidance still require it from time to time. However, they recover quickly and soon get back on track.

Getting results through others is one of the most challenging things for a new leader/manager to master. Even senior leaders sometimes experience situations where they provided the proper amount of leadership, yet the results were unsatisfactory.

So, how do we get things done the way we want them completed?

Through the years, I have achieved great results by motivating people to be accountable while accomplishing all of the tasks they are assigned. It wasn't always easy, however. I found I needed to sometimes act differently in order to achieve the desired results.

I have shared great conversations with a team member only to forget to follow up because I thought the task I assigned would be accomplished. I only found out later the task was never started and the team member never gave it a second thought once I left them alone.

I realized they didn't neglect what I wanted. Instead, the fault lay with me for failure to follow up.

The following steps will help you bring accountability to your organization.

1. Make sure team members understand what you want or expect.

2. Have them repeat back to you a description of what the task entails.

3. Make sure they understand all steps required to have a successful outcome.

4. Keep the team members you supervise accountable by checking back within a week to see what progress they are making.

I'm not talking about micro-managing. When you get back to someone, it is more about your support for them and what they are doing to accomplish the task. Assist them and clarify the steps without pressuring them. The value of checking back is the person can tell you about the steps they took as well as any difficulties or barriers they encountered. This allows you to step in and offer suggestions to help them complete the task.

Many times, we work in such chaotic, crisis-oriented environments where long-term plans or even short-term goals are placed on a back-burner where they are forgotten. We call this the tyranny of urgency.

There are situations where you need to take a more structured approach to get done what needs to be done. The reason is, when you ask people to do something for you or the organization, it should be of such importance it gets done. People will invariably treat you the way you allow them to treat you. They will try to teach you how to hold them accountable. Don't fall for it!

Being familiar and friendly with some of your people will produce an incredible team. Being familiar with others can lead them to not take you seriously.

This often results in them being less responsive than you want. By balancing your approach, a leader will gain wisdom, however, it can be a painful experience. When this happens, you may want to take another track.

One time, I asked one staff member to complete a very important project for the organization. The person was resistant to taking on the assignment because it would require a great deal of work and it might reveal some skills they lacked or weren't doing well.

Although we worked together a long time, whenever I came to this person with a request for information, she started to tell me she couldn't give me a time frame for completion nor could she even start on the task because of her current workload. Finally, I obtained the information I needed. However, it required more follow-up than I anticipated. This person was actually reluctant to do something included as part of their job description and well within their area of responsibility. I realized this might eventually become a personnel issue and result in corrective action needing to be taken. Therefore, I communicated through correspondence so there was proper documentation if this did turn into a personnel issue.

The following steps will help you create structure for a project or task and hold your people accountable:
- Tell them you will send an email describing exactly what task you want done.
- Lay out in writing any steps they should take.
- Create a time frame for them to complete the required task.

If you cannot supervise the task yourself, select another executive to oversee and hold the person accountable. Inform the person you select as supervisor and let them know you are holding them accountable for seeing the task to completion.

Let them both know the only reason things might change on the provided list is if there is a better idea to accomplish a step on the task list. Require the person to obtain an agreement first before proceeding on any new course of action. Let them know, under no circumstance will anyone else in the organization have the authority to change the directions provided unless you grant someone the specific authority.

I also provide the list of tasks with all the above requirement to the leader who usually supervises the person designated to accomplish the tasks. It is also important to let the person know your request is non-negotiable. Again, all these steps must be provided in writing.

This process works well when you find someone resisting to do what you want accomplished.

Your success as a leader relates to how well you guide the people you supervise.

It is important to understand whenever you have tension with an employee, the way a situation is handled has the goal of making your relationship with them better. Otherwise, it might make them bitter and they may leave you. Sometimes, you may decide it is better to dismiss them or replace them.

Why is it not a good idea to lead by compassion?

I have watched therapists attempt to lead from a therapeutic point of view and social workers lead from a case management or needs based perspective. It is always a good thing to use whatever other skills and perspectives you might possess as you grow into leadership. However, it is my point of view you should not replace the fundamentals of leadership with compassion.

While it is often necessary to have compassion, understanding, concern and many other traits with which we are blessed, it is not wise to have compassion as your primary focus.

An analogy would be an emergency worker coming onto an accident scene. What should be their priority? My perspective is they should assess the situation, define what the various problems might be and deal with the most pressing issue first. They would not go to everyone initially and console them. They would decide what is the greatest area of need and go to work triaging the situation.

In the case of an emergency worker situation, it is best to determine who needs treatment first. Also assess whether additional resources are needed, request those resources, then determine who should be the first person transported to hospital for more care than can be provided at the scene.

While leaders generally don't run into this types of crisis, the same concepts apply.

For example, let's imagine one of your funders wants an immediate response about a grant and the person who knows the most about the situation is on vacation or in the hospital.

What should be the leader's best response? In my opinion, it would be to assess the request from the funder. After looking at the request and the deadline given, determine whether there are enough other resources available to effectively answer the request. It would probably be wise to contact someone in the financial department and request key staff be available to answer questions from the funder.

Obviously, what the leader pays attention to first depends upon each unique situation. However, an effective leader will create a plan or contingency to solve a particular problem. Next will be a step I call circling back where leaders listen to their employees and assess any resistance so the leader can provide the appropriate assistance to help the affected employees reprioritize their job load to handle the emergency.

Once the problem is defined and a plan put in place, only then should the effective leader use compassion to emphasize his caring of the extra efforts people are going through to solve the issue or complete the funder's request. This may eventually reshape some of the plan, but overall, the leaders must make sure the problem is solved in a timely fashion and to the satisfaction of the funder.

Leading by compassion can be incredibly effective in some contexts. However, there are potential drawbacks or limitations which might make it less suitable in certain situations. Here are some reasons why leading by compassion might not always be the best approach. My experience shows that autocratic leaders and those who lead only with compassion are the least effective leaders.

Focusing on the compassionate leader who leads by being in touch with their feelings and the feelings of others first will, in most cases, lead to crisis, morale problems, low performance and decreased productivity. What sometimes gets lost first is the focus on performance and productivity which can lead an organization into financial crisis, loss of focus on the vision and the potential for losing outstanding staff.

The following are some explanations of what may happen if someone's primary focus is compassion as a leadership trait.

Perceived Weakness

Risk of being seen as lenient: If compassion is not balanced with accountability, it may be perceived as a sign of weakness or leniency. Employees might take advantage of a compassionate leader, leading to a lack of discipline or decreased productivity.

Decision-Making Challenges

Difficulty Making Tough Decisions: Compassionate leaders might struggle with making difficult decisions, such as layoffs or disciplinary actions, because they are more concerned with individuals' feelings.

Potential for Bias

Favoritism: Compassion can sometimes lead to favoritism if a leader is more empathetic towards certain employees, potentially causing resentment and division within the team.

Boundary Issues

Blurred professional boundaries: Excessive compassion can blur the lines between professional and personal relationships, leading to boundary issues and potentially affecting professional objectivity.

Resource Drain

Emotional exhaustion: Constantly leading with compassion can be emotionally draining for the leader, potentially leading to burnout.

Inconsistency

Inconsistent Application: Compassionate leadership might result in inconsistency if decisions are made based on individual circumstances rather than established policies and procedures.

Impeded Performance

Potential for Lower Performance Standards: If compassion is not paired with high expectations and accountability, it might lead to complacency and lower performance standards within the team.

Risk of Enabling Poor Behavior

Enabling Poor Performance: Compassionate leaders may inadvertently enable poor performance or behavior problems by being too forgiving and not addressing issues directly.

Balancing Compassion with Other Leadership Qualities

Some helpful hacks for the compassionate leader include the following:

Accountability: Ensure that compassion does not undermine accountability. Set clear expectations and hold team members responsible for meeting them.

Objectivity: Maintain objectivity and fairness in decision-making to avoid favoritism and ensure consistent treatment of all employees.

Boundaries: Establish and maintain professional boundaries to avoid the pitfalls of over-familiarity.

Resilience: Build resilience to manage the emotional demands of compassionate leadership without experiencing burnout.

Leading by compassion can be highly effective when combined with a balanced approach that includes accountability, clear communication, and professional boundaries. This combination can help create a supportive yet high-performing work environment.

The power of a crisis!

One of the greatest things you can do during a crisis is to change things.

A former Chief of Staff for then-President Barack Obama is credited with the following quote:

> *"You never let a crisis go to waste.*
> *And what I mean by that:*
> *It's an opportunity to do things*
> *that you did not think you could do before."*

Ron Emanuel

This is a powerful concept. If you are wanting to move forward or are taking over an organization and you face resistance, you may need to find a way to move beyond the resistance. This concept will do it for you.

You can do things with less resistance or friction such as:

- Invest time in building relationships.
- Take time to find out who they are and what their lives are about.
- Care for them.

In the early 1990s, I was asked to take over a drug and alcohol program for youth in an impoverished area of the coastal mountains of California. The program director I replaced was determined by the State of California to be out of compliance with state requirements. My job was to fix the complaints and to make things right with the probation officers who placed 12 youths from urban areas with challenging lives. Because the organization was not breaking even financially, another aspect of my job was to make it profitable once more by bringing the organization's bottom line back into the black.

On my arrival at the facility, even as I was pulling into a parking space at what used to be an old Stagecoach Hotel in the late 1800s, I noticed several government vans loading up youths for transport back to the county from which they were placed.

I quickly realized the major challenge ahead of me. I was in charge of a program from which all of the youth were being removed. In essence, I started with no clients for an organization with a tarnished reputation I needed to fix. The job also entailed fixing some long-term systemic problems involving probation offices from throughout the state of California. And all this had to be accomplished immediately!

My first thought was to meet with all the employees and see how they were doing. I needed to retain employees and I needed them to trust me. Since the town in which my new organization was located had a population of fewer than 100 people, there wasn't an abundance of qualified people from which I could draw fresh recruits.

Another issue, most of my employees were afraid of losing their jobs. They also did not want to serve under another knuckle-headed director like the one the company recently terminated. In fact, in the 16 months since the program opened, these employees suffered a succession of three agency directors.

I asked my administrative staff to help me set up appointments within the next 48 hours so I could meet with every employee and they could get to know me. I even traveled 70 miles to meet with a key employee whom I knew to be essential if I was going to be successful in turning the organization around.

Making sausage is never a perfect art form and neither are the ways we resolve a crisis. By the next month, the organization was able to retain more than 96 percent of its employees and we were able to welcome back many of our former clients and even a few new referrals for the future. From that day on until I was promoted to COO of this large organization, we enjoyed a full census and a strong effective staff which helped make a difference in the lives of the young boys entrusted to our care and treatment. Lives were once again being transformed, and leadership was no longer a problem with the organization.

Preventing professional misery

Leadership can be miserable, if you allow it. When you feel like you don't want to go to work tomorrow or you hate your job, it may revolve around an employee issue.

I founded a very successful organization and, at times, even I sometimes wanted to simply walk away from it. When I look back, it was usually because I was frustrated because I was not taking responsibility for what was happening in my own organization.

Generally, I found the situation required one of the following actions to move the organization forward:

1. Removing a problem employee
2. Realigning employees to better meet the needs of the organization
3. Creating better support for myself and my team members
4. Making the organization more efficient and effective
5. Implementing new standards

From time to time, it is wise to do some major work internally to develop a more effective paradigm to get yourself or the organization out of an untenable situation. If you think this is harsh advice, I challenge you to look at all the times you have been miserable and determine why. Misery will quickly rob your joy and some employees may need to be employed elsewhere.

Every organization has goals and the leader's job is to refine these goals, whether it be an organization's goal or a divisional goal. The leader's goal and every individual's goal is to make sure they and all the people they supervise are able to fully focus energy towards accomplishing the goal or goals related to the organization's success or profitability.

In the case of a CEO or Executive Director, your focus should be on the goals your organizations set or were set for you by a Board of Directors.

Most leaders have some control aspects embedded in their personality. Like all gifts, control can be overused. When control is overused, it usually becomes a negative in our lives. However, we do need to use authority to correct people who are off track. Those who have gone rogue must be persuaded to get back to doing the tasks they are required to complete.

In the absence of leadership, some people in the organization may take advantage and move themselves and other employees in a different direction.

Keeping your organization on track!

Leaders can train people to do their jobs and assign people leadership positions. However, leaders must continue to pour their own knowledge and experience into their people. Below are a few things to help you make headway in developing relationships with the people you supervise:

- Continue to have personal conversations with employees. Find out what they do or not do.
- When you train a person for another position, make sure they are clear this is training for the future and the leadership team will decide when there is a need to expand the position.
- Always respond to two areas affecting employees, these are the barriers which stop or slow down people from accomplishing their work goals and doing their tasks. Secondly, be aware of those things which bring down standards or make your organization less effective in accomplishing its goals.
- Address anything causing deviation within the organization.
- Address problems as soon as you possibly can!

CURIOSITY IS THE CORE OF LEADERSHIP

"I have no special talents.
I am only passionately curious."

Albert Einstein

Why is curiosity the key to leadership? This may sound weird to you, however, a thing we think is just a fun thing we do in life, being curious, might be at the core of leadership. If you research various leaders in industry and the nonprofit world, almost all leaders will have something to say about the power of curiosity. When I'm curious, I ask questions like: "Why would someone choose another organization over mine?" or "How can I double the size of our organization?"

I cannot remember asking a question and not receiving a helpful answer.

"Leadership is not about being in charge.
It is about taking care of those in your charge.

John C. Maxwell

Curiosity helps leaders better connect with their team, understand individual and collective needs as well as inspire innovation. Questions are far more important and powerful than statements!

A statement sometimes ends thinking.

Leaders connect best with people when we show interest in them or their work. When we combine curiosity with managing by wandering around, a leader can make great headway in forming solid relationships. I make it a personal discipline to be curious with all types of people, whether it be a sushi maker at a resort in Cabo San Lucas or a passenger sitting beside me on an airplane. I strike up conversations and often make great friends out of strangers. By being curious, I learned about the experiences of an American living in the south of Spain as well as what goes on in the daily work of a personal injury lawyer.

Curiosity is key to connecting with your team and future team members. It is also key to developing a network in the community, in the state and possibly national or internationally.

I believe a leader's future depends on curiosity.

I was conversing with a consultant friend and informed him a certain county was asking me whether I might take charge of a program nobody else wanted. I was hesitant since I did not like the way the program was designed. However, before I shut the door on an opportunity, I went to speak with a friend and asked his opinion.

"Caleb, tell me what you would do with this program?" I asked.

Caleb suggested this same program would work as part of a larger plan and recommended I should seriously consider taking it on.

"Mike, I think you're missing what this program could do for you," Caleb urged. "I believe you could use this program as a catalyst to get larger contracts down the road," he added.

He was right! I told the county I would do their program. It took two years to get the contract and implement it. However, what started out as a $100,000 per year contract ended up being a $400,000 contract per year. With the county's encouragement and financing, we were able to start a mental health services program for children in a way we were never able to do before!

> *"Stay committed to your decisions,*
> *but stay flexible in your approach.*
> *It's the curiosity to explore new ways*
> *that keeps a leader's strategy dynamic."*

> **Tony Robbins**

Your future as a leader depends on an active sense of curiosity!

I am convinced a question spurred by curiosity can be the catalyst for extraordinary innovation. It just takes the right question and you could soon be on the road to more innovations and answers to problems you are facing.

Do yourself a favor. Check out your biases. Yes, you have them. Everyone has biases, especially people who don't think they are biased.

In this context, I'm referring to judgments and conclusions we hold onto without a single challenge.

Not challenging our biases when we are making decisions or even when we are meeting new people is dangerous. Be mindful of how you are feeling and what you are thinking. Doing this often creates new opportunities when coupled with curiosity.

It seems the more educated and sophisticated we become, the more we miss the nuances of life. Usually and unfortunately, the highly educated among us head straight for the answers instead of asking great questions. Sometimes we lose out on what could be life-changing opportunities because we already think we have the solution for a problem before diagnosing it. We certainly wouldn't trust a doctor who did this, so why would we trust ourselves. Ask questions first! Then challenge your own conclusions.

To support what I am telling you, there is an article I found in the Harvard Business Review with the title, "Curiosity is as Important as Intelligence" written by Tomas Chamorro-Prezmuzic.

The premise of this article: Curiosity has a great deal to do with how successful people are. Curiosity and mindset are leading indicators and can even be used to predict the success of a leader.

Being curious is crucial!

"Leadership requires two things:
a vision of the world that does not yet exist
and the ability to communicate it.
Curiosity fuels both."

Simon Sinek

An organization with curiosity as an essential part of its culture will experience more success. I personally see curiosity as a strength when looking at complicated issues, especially when I want to engage my team to generate better answers. Curiosity is a familiar topic of study for academia and leaders in the field. All indications show curiosity contributes to personal and professional growth.

I know many young people in my own organization and a few others who go to Disneyland on a regular basis. They are always talking about some superpower the experience provides. Well, curiosity is one of the most powerful superpowers I've ever witnessed.

Here are three things you need to do to be a master at curiosity.

1. Leave your answers at home.
2. Be genuinely curious. Don't interrupt when you're getting a genuine response. Better yet think of a great question and continue to listen.
3. Use your curiosity to connect with others and solve problems by asking thoughtful, open-ended questions which encourage dialogue and deeper understanding.

"Curiosity will conquer fear even more than bravery will."

James Stephens

"We keep moving forward, opening new doors and doing new things because we're curious and curiosity keeps leading us down new paths."

Walt Disney

"Just because you are the leader
doesn't mean you have all the answers.
Stay curious. Ask questions.
The best ideas come from collective curiosity."

Indra Nooyi

Questions for Problem-Solving:

Here are some questions I've found to be effective when solving problems. Direct these questions to the people whom you believe can give you insight.

Understanding a Problem:

Can you help me understand the root cause of this issue?

What are the key factors contributing to this problem?

How does this problem impact our overall goals?

Exploring Solutions:

What solutions have you tried so far and what were the outcomes?

What resources or support do we need to address this issue effectively?

Who else might have valuable insights or experience to help us solve this issue?

Considering Alternatives:

What are the potential risks and benefits of each solution?

How can we approach this problem from a different perspective?

What would an ideal solution look like?

Implementation:

What steps should we take to implement this solution?

How will we measure the success of our solution?

What could go wrong?

How can we mitigate these risks?

Questions for Connecting with Others:

When you want to find out more from colleagues about those they lead, ask these questions:

Building Rapport:

Can you tell me more about your background and experiences?

What are you most passionate about in your work?

What do you enjoy doing outside of work?

Understanding Perspectives:

How do you view this situation?

What are your thoughts on the current challenges we're facing?

What experiences have shaped your perspective on this issue?

Encouraging Collaboration:

What ideas do you have for improving your (or our) current approach?

How can we support each other to achieve our goals?

What skills or strengths do you bring to the table that we can leverage?

Deepening Engagement:

What motivates you to do your best work?

How can we create an environment where everyone feels valued and heard?

What are your long-term goals, and how can we help you achieve them?

PERFORMANCE MANAGEMENT

Have you ever wondered how to get quicker results to accomplish the goals you set? Do you want to continuously grow your organization to the next level or beyond? Goal setting and goal achieving seem to be distant cousins at times when we ask ourselves those two questions. However, recently I've discovered a simple and more effective way of getting the results I desire. This method is by far more successful than any other method I've tried.

This epiphany occurred when I came across the book *Measure What Matters* written by venture capitalist L. John Dooer, one of the first investors in Google when the company started in the proverbial one-car garage in Palo Alto, Calif.

Dooer reportedly invested $12 Million for a 12 percent share of ownership in Google Inc. The company, now part of Alphabet Inc., currently has a market cap of more than $2.14 Trillion. Apparently, Dooer is one of those guys capable of seeing around corners.

Google Inc. was founded in 1998 by Larry Page and Sergey Brin and they were just trying to get their business off the ground. Dooer, who previously worked for Intel before joining the venture capital firm Kleiner Perkins, learned early in his career about a performance management program called Objectives and Key Results, most often shortened to the acronym OKR, which virtually transformed Silicon Valley in the early 1980s.

The rest is history!

What is OKR and how does it work?

It's a pretty simple process. You have your Objectives or Goals and you have your Key Results which, when added together, should equal your expected Outcomes.

This is how OKRs work!

I've used OKRs to grow every area of my agency. OKRs help simplify your organization's forward growth and development. I've used OKRs to implement complex contracts, to double the size of a division and to bring everyone together to accomplish a new organizational goal.

One of my divisions was just beginning to move into the specialty field of mental health.

I needed to break down a very complex contract and begin to implement steps to achieve the desired results. I invited six of my key people to sit around a table and none of us had a pre-conceived plan on how to move forward.

As I went around the room, I asked everyone what he or she believed should be our overriding goal. This goal should always be somewhat extravagant. We came up with, "We will become the largest provider of specialty mental health services in northern California.

Above this statement, I wrote a single word.

OBJECTIVE

"To be the largest provider of specialty mental services in northern California"

Below this heading, I wrote the following:

KEY RESULTS   **RESPONSIBILITY**

Then, we began as a group to work through the steps of reorienting staff members who would most likely work in this section of our new services. This included informing each of them regarding the scope of our new contract.

We then created a chart to hang in our board room so everyone could become familiar with all the new acronyms.

We also began to research what services we could charge and determine the appropriate rates.

Each Key Result was assigned to a specific team member or group of people. This was all accomplished during our first meeting. We also set a goal of having each of these items completed within a month even though this would take us well into the Christmas season. In 30 days, we linked each Objective with the appropriate Key Results identified.

At the next meeting after Christmas, we set up three additional Key Results, remembering each Key Result must always be related to the overriding Objective.

As you can see, this process continually brings up the most important issues needing attention in order for an organization to move forward.

The Objective gives us a horizon of where we are going and a Goal to identify the ultimate accomplishment. Having a grand goal begins to put into motion what resources are necessary, what staffing levels are needed and what skills or capacity is required. The real power in having a grand goal is we were able to quickly define the layers of accomplishment needed to achieve them.

Why should you use OKRs?

The beauty of this process is once you have established a goal, you add three to five items to move you towards the goal. After you set a completion date for the first three to five items and complete them successfully, then you add in the next three to five items in need of completion.

I like to keep this process simple. Have an overarching goal and three to five steps needed to complete in a short time frame. This could be within a week or a month.

Generally, I prefer the time frame to be no longer than three months if the task cannot be completed within a single month. When using OKRs, you will discover as I did, you accomplish reaching goals faster and achieve more buy-in from team members than ever before.

Please do yourself a favor and read John Dooer's book or listen to his video on YouTube.

As a leader of a nonprofit organization, it is my opinion you should be constantly on the lookout for new opportunities. I'm not urging you to take every opportunity. However, it is important to be aware your organization needs to be constantly in motion. Opportunities are one way to keep stimulating this motion going forward.

Those agencies who rely only on past success will find themselves desperate and not able to fulfill their future mission in the ways they wish. They will also not be able to hire top talent because of their constant lack of funding. Worse yet, many of their team members will leave due to their lack of hope for the organization's future as well as their own.

The executive director of a successful organization must regularly look at four things:

What is the organization's future?

What are the future possibilities in our field?

How will the organization position itself for the future?

Where do we want to take our organization?

Jim Collins describes this in his book *Good to Great* as the ultimate question: What is your big hairy audacious goal?

Some leaders are hesitant to take risks. Usually, they do not want to experience the stress of a possible failure while tackling a new venture.

Is this a realistic position for a successful leader to take? I believe leaders should be courageous and have this as their mindset: I will do the best I can to plan and assess the new opportunities by planning and strategizing for the success of our organization's future ventures. If this doesn't work out, don't tell yourself you are a loser or let others label you as one. Instead, look at all the goals you fell short of and ask, "What did I (we) learn from this?

Getting positive results with OKRs is one of the easiest things I have ever done.

Most organizations create their goals annually and hope they can accomplish what they know is important for their organization. However, most of us have difficulty meeting such lofty goals and end up trying to achieve the very same goals year after year.

Unfortunately, for those organizations not growing or advancing, eventually they lose any ability to effectively serve their clients and most will end up just getting by with, quite frankly, only meager results.

However, OKRs make this process very simple. You create your ultimate goal — in the words of Jim Collins your "big hairy audacious goal" — as your Objective.

Your goal, as ours once was, might be to achieve status as the largest childcare service program in your county or state. It could be you want to have the finest equine program for youth in your local area. You may even want to become a thought leader in a particular subject. Whatever it is, it needs to be something of a stretch. Something which would be a great achievement if you accomplished it.

If you wanted to be the largest childcare program in your county, this is your Objective.

The next step is to begin to break your goal down into numbers. For example, increase marketing by using social media. Start with at least one new post released each week.

The next step might be to start blogging. The purpose of blogging is twofold. One, it demonstrates to readers you know your business and are a recognized expert in the field. Two, it also helps drive families, referral sources and other interested people to your website.

If your website is not in good shape, fixing it might be one of your intermediate goals to help realize your objective.

For example:

Objective

Be the largest childcare program in Sacramento County!

Key Results

1. Know the requirements of starting a program or multiple programs.
2. Estimate what this objective might cost to accomplish.
3. Build a budget.
4. Design the marketing.

In my organization, we have four or five people who meet every week. Many of our key results are set to be achieved within a two-week period. Although we sometimes have goals requiring three months to complete, I much prefer to work with a sense of urgency.

Much of what you do is likely to be whatever is reasonable. If you are a one- or two-person operation, it will likely take you longer to accomplish some of your goals. However, the faster you complete your key results, the sooner you can hire more people to help realize your goals!

Constraint Theory:

It is leadership's job to make sure organizations are performing effectively on a regular basis.

The following are things you can do to turn your organization into a high performing machine and continue in a state of high performance.

1. Measure what you do.

2. Teach your employees about Constraint Theory.

Any system you use or create is bound to have constraints. Constraints are problems either external (outside of your organization) or internal (problems within your organization). Any system or best practice will work until it bumps up against the constraints. The solution is to know what problems you have and solve them in the right order. Find out what is limiting you and work on solving those problems.

Make sure you look at problems from every angle or perspective. You may think you know the constraint only to find some other issue is actually causing the constraint. Being creative and thinking outside the box will solve many of your constraints.

For the leader of a nonprofit, Constraint Theory rises from the context of management principles focusing on identifying and addressing the most critical limiting factor or constraint which prevents the organization from achieving its goals, particularly in terms of mission impact, resource allocation or operational efficiency. Constraint Theory emphasizes systematic identification and improvement to eliminate the constraint. By identifying constraints, you will achieve better performance and improve your results.

You can use Constraint Theory by:

Identifying the Constraint: This could be a lack of funding, limited staff capacity, inadequate volunteer engagement, outdated technology or inefficient processes. For a nonprofit, the constraint might often be related to resources or external factors hindering program delivery.

Exploring the Constraint: Once identified, the organization should focus on maximizing the effectiveness and efficiency of the factors contributing to the constraint.

For instance, if funding is a constraint, the leader could prioritize fundraising efforts or reallocate existing funds.

Subordinating Other Activities: Aligning other aspects of the organization to support the identified constraint. For example, if volunteer engagement is a constraint, other departments might shift their focus to provide more support for volunteer recruitment and retention.

Eliminating this constraint can be accomplished by removing volunteer activity entirely or by obtaining other resources, restructuring programs or advocating for policy changes.

When dealing with multiple constraints, the constant must be this: Once one constraint is resolved, repeat the process to find and address the next most significant constraint.

Looking for constraints may seem like a lot of work. Usually, however, it isn't hard to find a constraint. If you ask employees what things they would improve, they will tell you. If you have errors in certain departments and you need to eliminate those errors, make this happen.

As a nonprofit leader, Constraint Theory is a way to strategically focus on key issues most hindering your organization's ability to achieve its mission. You can do this by ensuring your efforts and resources are directed where they will have the greatest impact. You will always have constraints. In fact, the more abundant your systems become, the more complex your operations will be. Complexity compounds errors as well as constraints.

Remember, your job as a leader is to solve problems!

If you have a management team or are creating one, implement into the culture their primary duty is to get results. Your leadership team needs to know and be reminded their first priority is to solve problems limiting your organization and its employees. Your first priority should be to obtain the results you and your people believe are important for your agency to continue to serve clients and thrive in the future.

You need to include results for the benefit of your clients while obtaining results in fulfilling your mission. So often, leaders of nonprofits take a soft approach. Results are secondary and accountability is nonexistent. If you want your organization to survive and thrive, you'll need to accomplish your goals.

Do the hardest thing first. When I say this, I am talking about taking the hardest thing you do and turn it into the easiest thing you do. This is more than a cliché. It is an attitude that will bring you great success.

For example, the hardest thing that 90 percent of foster programs do is recruit families. I took this as a challenge. I studied, researched and implemented recruiting efforts we use consistently. Eventually, we hit new highs in recruiting.

In fact, I took what we learned from recruiting and turned it into a virtual training which is helping agencies throughout Canada and the United States recruit families for foster care. I spoke at national conferences on this topic throughout the United States and Canada. We also created systems designed to let families know what we were doing during the entire recruiting and onboarding process.

Always have a plan for what you are doing the next day. When you show up for work, you need to have two or three things you are working on to move your organization forward.

Too many leaders allow the tyranny of the urgent to take up their valuable time. This can happen and usually we believe we are doing the right thing by paying attention to the urgent. Most of the time, however, somebody else can handle some of these urgent issues to allow the leader time to work on the organization and take it to new heights.

Move quickly in talking with people about areas of contention. When there are problems, define the problem and move on to a solution quickly.

The power of creating narratives!

Throughout a leader's career, they will invariably find a need to create narratives. For example, when COVID hit, my team's thoughts turned to how will foster parents react to the concept of not only parenting a child placed in their home, but becoming a teacher or, at very least, a teacher's aide so the child could continue to receive an education.

In general, our foster youths present some challenges with behavior and education. On top of this, many foster youths have special needs when it comes to learning. During COVID, by March of 2020, almost all of our recreation programs and opportunities were completely shut down.

However, our heroic foster parents stayed the course with support and great leadership from our division leaders and social workers who remained on the front lines.

When I heard the Archdiocese of New York was closing their private schools, I sensed California would be next. I put together a letter to our foster parents telling them we were in for a rough time. The communication was straight forward and so were the offers of support we communicated to our parents.

My focus was to keep all of our children in placement because there was nowhere else to move them. Child Welfare Service Departments in every county told their staff members to work from home. This meant we could no longer meet in person to discuss the needs of the children in our care. Therefore, our own staff stepped up to handle any crisis.

Unlike ours, some other foster care agencies took a fortress mentality. They ceased to recruit new homes or take on any new placements. Many of their parents did not want to take in new placements because they might have an increased risk of exposure to COVID. Leadership of those other agencies appeared to commiserate with the parents' feelings instead of supporting them to take in these children due to a sense of need and commitment.

Well, we didn't want to go this direction. We wanted our families to not give up on the children in their care. I wanted our staff to focus on what was possible, not on the obstacles and barriers. My leadership team and I set about creating a narrative for our own staff as well as the foster parents. During the time of COVID, when everything was shut down, our agency hit three new all-time highs in recruiting foster parents. We maxed out our counseling contracts and we lost less than two percent of our parents. Most importantly, we kept 98 percent of our assigned children. We were able to stabilize those children and support their foster parents which made us a much tighter community. We continually communicated everything we were told about COVID by county and state programs. Transparency helped us create a strong narrative about standing beside our foster parents and working closely with them.

Because of our messaging, the commitment of our staff and their integrity, the foster care families and children trusted us. Together, we were able to make it through the roughest time many of us ever experienced.

The narrative we created was real, supportive and appreciative of the hard work accomplished by our parents. We came through COVID stronger than ever and prepared for our future.

SIGMOID CURVES AHEAD

What the heck is a Sigmoid Curve? It sounds like a fishing lure. However, it is one of the most poignant visual signs of success and allows a CEO and other executive leaders to understand growth and its stages. A Sigmoid Curve, also known as an S-shaped curve, is a mathematical function whose graph has a characteristic S-shape. It is commonly used to model growth and change over time in various fields like biology, demography and artificial neural networks. The Sigmoid Curve starts with slow growth, then accelerates, reaches a maximum and eventually slows down, often plateauing or declining.

Diagram of a Sigmoid Curve

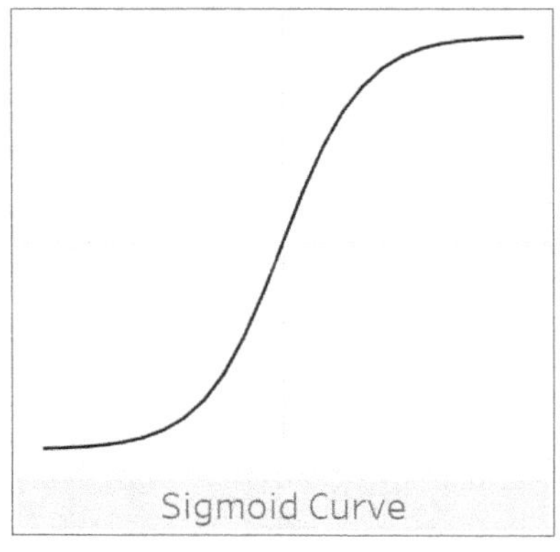

When I first saw this visual concept, it was life changing. Great concepts impact me because I constantly look for concepts and ideas to turn into presentations. All business ideas follow the course of the Sigmoid Curve. The first stage of curvature is the moment we start a business or organization.

The first year after I started a foster family agency, we served approximately 15 families and our gross revenue was less than $1 Million for the entire year. At this point, I believed we needed to have at least one other revenue stream to expand our agency more quickly as well as balance out the highs and lows of the original service we offered.

I didn't know what other venture I would try next, yet there were some guardrails to guide me. It needed to fit within our mission and require skills my staff could easily implement with our current capacity. It also needed to be something with a small startup cost.

We needed to be able to replicate this service in our contingent counties. It needed to involve fewer regulations or constraints than our initial enterprise. It was while attending a state association meeting for our industry when a profound idea struck! I suddenly realized what service I needed to create.

We needed a counseling center. I was holding onto some financial reserves and decided to invest in our future. The idea came to me as I was listening to leaders of larger agencies talk about an array of services they offered.

After I heard them, I realized we did not have the education and training necessary to lead this new service. However, I knew this new service was funded better and by a different division of the government which operated with fewer regulations. These things were important to me at the time. The service I originally developed, foster care, did not have a consistent Cost of Living Allowance. In fact, the state has only granted four Cost of Living Adjustments during the past 25 years.

I knew we had to grow and selected the mental health field in which to provide services.

Well, I was not familiar with counseling and mental health services so I hired a consultant. Our next steps were to talk with local county mental health leaders and ask them for a contract. We received a contract for $400,000 per year for 3 years. To date we have been serving in this area for almost 20 years. Our experience in counseling serves as a great example of the Sigmoid Curve. The Sigmoid Curve starts out almost flat and then slowly begins to rise.

In this First Stage, you're typically in the process of developing your

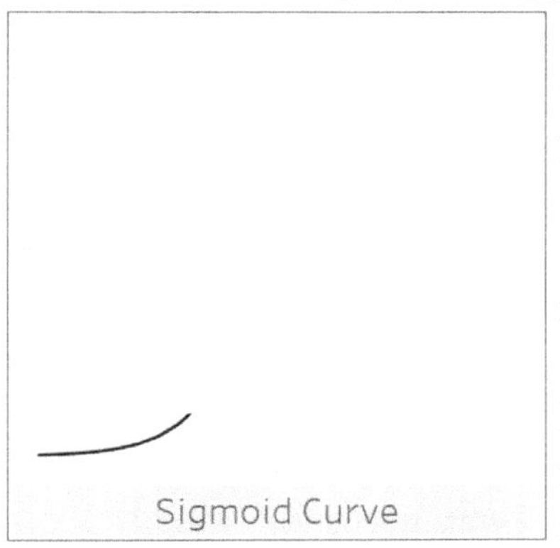

services. You begin to experiment with different strategies and try to find your place in the market. Growth is usually slow because the business is still establishing its customer base and refining its offerings. Growth at this stage is typically gradual.

It's not unusual to find you need to make significant investments in research, development, and personnel as well as infrastructure. This First Phase is critical for laying the foundation for future growth.

When we started our mental health clinic, we had to find a supervising clinician, subordinate clinicians, a place to provide services, hiring billing personnel and find clients. This was part of our plan and we had a pretty good idea of how to proceed. It did make it easier on us and probably saved us several years of struggle by hiring a consultant. We began to make progress and after about nine months, our two clinicians saw as many clients as they could.

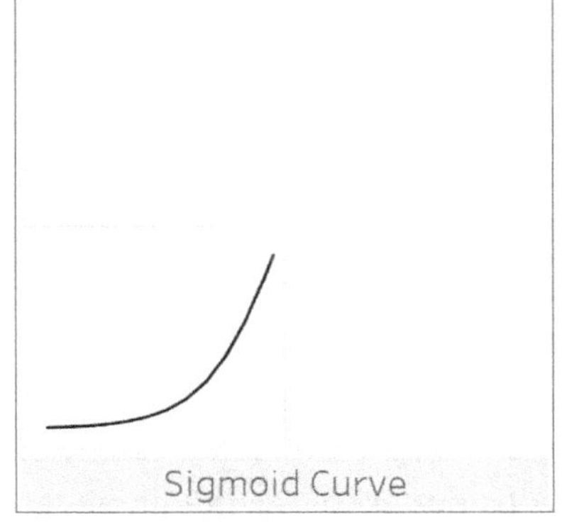

When the line goes up during the Second Stage, this is generally due to a lot of excitement for the new service. Remain hopeful and enjoy this success. Success also means you are able to provide additional services to new people and see more lives change. Many times this second stage can be classified as a time of rapid growth. This is the stage when you also will need an abundance of energy from your staff.

Your services will soon begin to gain acceptance in the community. You will probably see rapid growth because you are advertising and the market conditions are turning your way. You may find people who want to deal with your organization rather than your competitors.

You might find your organization scaling up during this time. Many times, your funders find they like what you are doing and begin to do more business with you or award grants or donations at a higher level to see more of the services you deliver. Scaling up can mean hiring more employees, increasing production, and possibly expanding faster than you thought into new markets or regions. You may also find your profits or margins are increasing. Market share may increase and you may see a faster rate of growth than you initially expected. Your growth may well surpass the rate of growth during your initial start-up stage.

The Third stage — Maturity:

Eventually you're going to be good in your new area of service. You may find you can do more things than what was initially expected of you. Learning how to provide new services isn't as challenging as it once might have been.

As your program matures, you may find your rate of learning things slows down. This is when to begin fine tuning your services. The Maturity stage represents a leveling off. This phase represents the top of your growth for a period. At the flattening part of the Sigmoid curve, this indicates a phase where growth stabilizes.

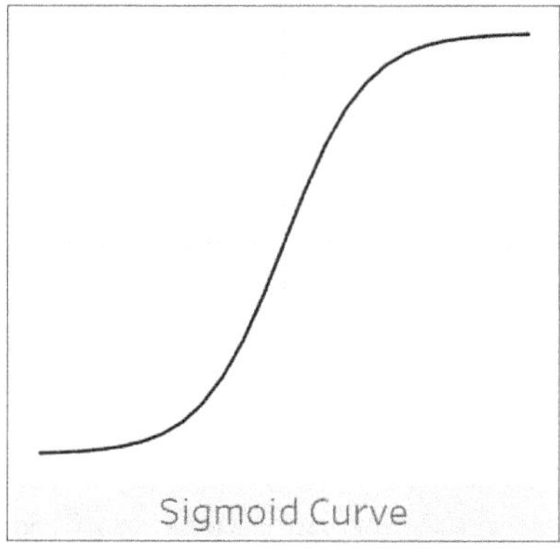

Maturity means the growth rate stabilizes as the market becomes saturated. At this stage, we usually were more comfortable and things were once again predictable.

I led divisions where their growth stayed steady or grew for more than 15 years. I also led others where the stabilization level was much shorter. I was never secure when maturity was reached. I like to have peace of mind and a small amount of anxiety. However, to me, not growing means any disruptions or economic issues can mean possible disaster if I don't have robust and steady revenue streams.

When maturity is reached, you may find a decline in some of your services, especially if new competition arises or funding changes or the market evolves in other ways.

This is my reason for embracing constant innovation or diversification. Innovation and diversification help to avoid decline. They can also kick start a new growth phase in older services or new revenue streams coming from innovation. This is the main reason most successful organizations diversify services.

> *"Don't compare yourself with anyone in this world.*
> *If you do so, you are insulting yourself.*
> *Stay curious, stay driven by your own desire*
> *to learn and improve."*

Bill Gates

> *"Vulnerability is the birthplace of innovation, creativity, and change.*
> *It all starts with the willingness to be curious*
> *and ask the tough questions."*

Brené Brown

It is important to constantly assess what stage you and your organization are at. If you are in this second phase, you should be looking at your next actions to revive your key services. If your service base is dwindling, you may want to add an iteration or begin a new service to continue support for the organization. At this stage, it is also important to start something new or reinvigorate your current service if you desire continued growth.

The third phase is one of growth or even one of slight decline. The plateau phase in business tells us no organization or service lasts forever. No growth trajectory is eternal. The inevitable journey of every business, organization or service has a rise, a plateau and — without strategic intervention — a decline. The Sigmoid Curve is more than a mathematical concept. It is a stark reality of the business world.

> *"The sigmoid curve not only captures the essence of growth and decay, but also tells the story of how change happens — slowly at first, then rapidly, and finally leveling off."*

David Sumpter
in *Soccermatics*

CREATING, NOT COMPETING

How to be the best in the long-term

I believe most top leaders need also to be chief marketers. Sharing this belief will propel you ahead of 95 percent of the organizations in your space. I use this approach repeatedly, as have other business organizations. However, only a few non-profits truly understand the concept.

The concept of Creating, Not Competing begins like this:

Start by observing and determining what the best organizational leaders in your industry are doing. This can be in the areas of marketing, business practices, delivery of services, culture or anything else you might decide is your immediate focus of interest.

Then work towards matching the very best in their efforts. A great leader would be wise to differentiate services in such a fashion to begin capturing more of the market because your organization's way of providing services is viewed as far superior.

After you match the efforts of your competitors, work on surpassing them by continual innovation. For example, there are several hundred foster care agencies in California. When I first started my agency, our primary goal was simply survival. During my first three months, I learned half of our clients would be leaving within the next three months. I became anxious because we were not yet starting to receive a flow of clients from the counties with whom I wanted to work.

One thing I learned from this difficult period was to listen to others in the field.

I also listened to my staff and did two important things.

1. I looked at what our organization could do differently from any other agency. This helped create a natural barrier for those parents who wanted to access another agency's services.

2. I designed our organization with as few barriers as possible to those who desired to work with our organization.

Example:

One of my social workers asked me early on whether we would charge potential foster parents for the cost we incurred in obtaining their FBI and DOJ background reports. One alternative, and some agencies were already doing this, once a person or couple was approved as a foster parent, they would receive reimbursement for any expenses connected with obtaining these clearances.

One staffer asked me what we should do.

"Why is this important to you?" I responded.

"Well, in my opinion, any barriers new potential foster parents must overcome will keep us from recruiting the foster parents we need," was her reply.

I considered her reference point was for the betterment of our clients and realized she was right.

As a result, very early on, I decided our organization would pay for any expenses for potential foster parents who passed an initial interview. Doing this eliminated any reluctance, especially from those parents who wanted to start the process immediately. It also meant our process was better than what was available from most other agencies. We were creating without competing. Having better ideas is much better than competing head-to-head.

For this reason, I want to know what the best organizations are doing so we can surpass them and put them in our rear-view mirror. I also consider myself the chief marketer for my organization.

What exactly does this mean? Am I saying I need to do all the marketing? Absolutely not.

However, I freely admit I am naturally better at doing things other than overseeing the organization's marketing. Yet, I still consider marketing to be the one place I must have oversight control because marketing is so critical in fueling our financial engine. As Peter Drucker so clearly communicated, "No margin, no mission"!

The CEO is responsible for the financial health of his or her organization. When an organization does not have financial sustainability, they won't be open long, or they will become a mere shadow of their vision!

"People who don't take risks generally make
about two big mistakes a year.
People who do take risks generally make about two big mistakes a year."

Peter Drucker

To me, this means when a leader oversees marketing, he or she will also need to innovate and try new things. This also means the leader may make a few mistakes or experience fewer positive results than he or she desires. However, it doesn't mean a leader must give up making choices.

Many nonprofits, however, don't have much competition. For example, an animal refuge center is usually the only one in its entire region. This type of program may not directly compete with equivalent organizations. However, they do compete for available donations in the same region as many other nonprofit agencies. Competing for donor funds is hard work and thus requires innovation and differentiation. If you are in a competitive environment, there are practical philosophical views you can claim and some practical things you can do.

Becoming competitive!

1. Determine what the public expects from a program such as yours. To do this properly, you may need to look outside your local area and think regionally or nationally. Every industry or specialty has accepted rules and ways of doing things. You can look at other animal programs, health programs, drug and alcohol programs, etc. Find out what is required of your specific field or industry. This may require you to also become an expert on regulations governing your particular area of interest.

   1. Find the best organizations in your space. You'll want to know who the best is so you can discover what has made them the best in the field. Research the top two or three organizations in your field. Begin to create a strategy to meet the services at the level of the best organizations in your field. Your strategy should include what you need to do and how you will get it done. Matching the best in your industry can happen quickly. Most of this depends on you and your leadership. At times, it will also depend

s on the quality of your staff as well as your level of funding.

2. Create a plan to match the best level of service you can find. This may sound confusing since earlier I advised you to be "creating, not competing." I understand your dilemma, however, to reach the level where you are truly "creating, not competing," you must have in place a solid foundation. Once you identify what the leading agencies are doing, you must compare your own systems, values and philosophies against theirs. As you do this assessment, make a list of the regulations, services and expectations of your particular industry. This is the process that will eventually lead you to be the leading organization of your type. Be patient with yourself. It takes time. However, you can speed up the process by having a plan and a strategy. Understanding every decision made at this point will help create a better future for your organization.

3. Once you've achieved the level of the best of other organizations similar to yours, now it is time to blow the doors off your competition. Put them in your rear-view mirror as you start creating. When you truly achieve being one of the best, you will generally find more funding, greater commitment and additional buy-in from your employees as you begin providing superior quality in those services you deliver.

MARKETING YOUR ORGANIZATION

Somewhere along the way, good leaders take responsibility for the organization's marketing. Either you've grown and certain parts of your business require fresh marketing or maybe you need to start marketing so more people will know about you.

It is your job to get in front of potential clients. It is not the client's job to find you.

In order to be successful in marketing, you must have good data. You also need to analyze your actions so you have a better idea of what you should do more as well as what you should do less.

Please know, I certainly don't do all the marketing. I usually meet with the people most responsible for marketing, approve purchases and ask what results we achieved from our last marketing event or investment. However, I do want to know how effective is our marketing. Why are we using the media outlets we use? What are our marketing goals?

I usually designate a group of leaders in my agency as the Creative Marketing Group. As CEO, I am included in this group. Membership is based primarily on meritocracy, meaning truth and the best ideas always win. At least in this group.

I led an organization with no revenue to more than $15 Million in annual gross revenue. Being familiar with marketing tools, technology and branding helped me to grow an organization.

However, I want fresh information. I also want everyone on our committee to think for themselves. Succession planning requires everyone has knowledge and is able to apply the principles which are making us successful. When we do this consistently, the best outcome is everyone thinks and researches and brings new ideas to a meeting.

Thinking is something I foster and encourage. Ideas different from my own are always welcome and will be considered on their merits. I often ask participants in our meetings to tell me what they know about what other agencies are doing. What opportunities are available to us? What else should we be doing?

When I talk about marketing, I'm talking specifically about making our services available to stakeholders who need what we offer. It also involves doing the necessary research to get the results we desire.

Leaders can't think of everything when making decisions. However, they do need to think through every possible scenario and contingency to prevent as many unpleasant surprises as possible! When we decided to expand into another geographical area, we did our research. We looked at potential sites for our next regional office and tried to obtain our best assessment of the potential market.

Believe me when I say your location will have a lot to do with the success of your agency. When we decided on our last move, we made up our criteria through research and input from data. Our goals were to have:

1. A larger population base. For almost 20 years, we were located in a rural area of northern California composed of three counties with a combined population of about 300,000 people. We wanted our next office to be in an area with a population of between 500,000 to 1,000,000 people located within an hour of the new office.

2. We wanted to still be located in a rural/urban area so we could continue serving small communities even as we took advantage of proximity to a larger urban community.

3. We wanted to be where several contiguous counties could use our services since our service array includes foster care as well as transitional housing. Our research established what various counties were doing for foster care services and how many children we projected to serve. We looked at the same type of data for transitional housing.

4. We also desired familiarity with the community where we would place our new office. We wanted to know and be familiar with the cultures and ethnicities of the area as well as the challenges of recruiting employees. Interestingly, we decided on the town where I was raised. Our new home base county was contiguous to six other counties. We were planting our office 45 minutes away from a major city with a population of more than 500,000. We were also

90 minutes away from other population centers with a combined population of 1.5 million.

Once we made our selection based on these criteria, we received assurances from the county targeted for our relocation that they indeed wanted us to be there. We also sought confirmation from surrounding contiguous counties of their desire for us to open an office nearby.

Why competition isn't important to me

> *"You do not rise to the level of your goals.*
> *You fall to the level of your systems."*

James Clear

As you might have noticed, I didn't mention any competition in this new area of service. Let me explain why competition is not as important to me now as it was when I started my organization.

I believe in systems. Systems and standards make you great and keep you at the top.

In every new area our agency moves into, we have become number 1 or number 2 in the region because we are relentless when it comes to quality and service.

Every client who comes to us in need deserves our very best! Having systems as the tool for quality means we increase the number of delivered services by improving and following our tested and proven systems.

Let's address another area of competition. Many colleagues in the childcare industry wrestle with the idea of competing with friends or former workmates. My question to them is this:

Who pays your mortgage or rent?

Some people have the philosophy, "We are all in this together."

In my mind, however, "being in this all together" generally means we should not do anything aggressive or different from what the competition does. To do this is to be coerced rather than to search for quality.

I've shared more information with my competitors than any other organizational leader. I even taught them how to recruit foster parents. I spent hours developing a presentation on this topic only to find leaders of other agencies unappreciative of my efforts. In retrospect, they were often oblivious to the very knowledge needed to benefit and grow their own organizations. I also realized some of this reaction came from my desire to have other leaders respect and like me. In most cases, this was a waste of my time.

I gladly mentor or help anyone who needs assistance. However, I will not do this if the price is to be disrespected or unappreciated.

In the child services space, it is popular in some areas for agencies to show up at the same events, dress and look the same in presentations and not rock the boat.

Not everyone participates at this level. However, there is enough conformity so anyone considering foster parenthood looks at the assorted agencies and thinks they're all the same.

It is important to differentiate even if your organization shares space with other organizations in your community. The very best nonprofits should tell the world why they are the best!

Of course, this must be done with humility and tact.

Nonprofits can market effectively by employing a variety of strategies which are cost-effective and impactful.

Here are some key approaches:

Leverage social media: Social media is the most important platform we use. Daily newspapers are mostly nonexistent anymore and telephone books are limited in their usefulness. Both of these traditional advertising platforms are expensive, as is the television market.

Social media is a powerful tool for reaching a wide audience. In fact, on most social media platforms you typically are able to choose the exact demographic you believe would be most receptive to learning about your nonprofit agency.

Social media also allows you to be the editor and curator of the content you want to create. You should use these platforms to share stories, updates and information about your cause and needs. You can easily use engaging content such as videos, images and infographics to help you gain visibility and attract supporters.

Social Media Marketing:

Nonprofits extensively use platforms such as Facebook, Instagram, Twitter, LinkedIn and even TikTok to reach a broader audience. It's cost-effective and offers the potential for content to go viral, increasing visibility.

Content Marketing and Storytelling:

Effective storytelling is crucial for nonprofits. By sharing compelling stories about your agency's work and the people it helps, you will connect emotionally with your audience. This can include blog posts, newsletters, videos and podcasts. Content marketing helps in educating the public, sharing success stories and keeping donors and volunteers engaged and informed.

Finding someone in your organization or hiring someone specifically to handle content marketing is an important asset necessary for your organization. Producing quality content such as blogs, articles, reports or white papers will quickly establish your organization as a thought leader in its field. Creating your own content also attracts media attention and boosts credibility.

Use social media:

Utilize the various social media platforms strategically in order to reach and engage with your key supporters in different age groups. This involves not only posting regular updates but also engaging in conversations and building an on-line community.

Platforms change often so assess which platform will best meet your needs.. Don't be afraid to experiment. Once you see people are interested in a particular platform, pursue why they are interested in it and determine how you might benefit from its use. You can also find out what stories, ads and requests generate the best results for your organization by doing A-B testing. Simply use different content, leads and media to see which message, A or B, attracts the most interest.

Develop valuable and relevant content to appeal to your audience. This could be in the form of blogs, videos, newsletters or infographics to tell your story as well as the impact of your work.

Videos and Podcasts

Videos and podcasts — sometimes called vodcasts — are now in the price range of most nonprofit organizations. It is important, however, to assess three things before you purchase the necessary production equipment:

Decide what to communicate and with whom you want to hear or see your messages. What message is most appropriate for each audience?

Decide what social media platform you want to use and be able to explain why.

Construct various methods for people to respond to your messages, whether it is through a link to a website or through an application they need to download in order to donate. It is a good thing to define what success should like before you start any marketing campaign.

Developing an Attractive and Functional Website!

A well-designed website is crucial for any nonprofit. It should be user-friendly, informative and updated regularly with news, events and success stories. It is essential for you to include a donation option prominently on your home page for everyone who lands there.

Understanding your audience will help you better address their needs, preferences and how they like to receive information. Tailoring your message to your audience is crucial for engagement.

We were recreating a website and we thought we had the right demographics. We inserted new pictures thinking we were covering the diversity within our foster parents and the youth we were serving. However, we were surprised by feedback received from a focus group we engaged to critique what we were doing. We discovered we were leaving out a large stakeholder population. When we saw one of the stakeholder's comment we were not being diverse enough, we called her and asked for more information.

"Well, I am a single Hispanic woman and you are not representing me in your pictures."

She was right. We were including children, youth and couples. However, nowhere in our message did we include a true representation of the true diversity contained in our current foster parent base.

Know your target audience!

It is important to know your target audience including their needs, preferences and how they prefer to receive information. Tailoring your message to your audience is crucial for engagement.

To be successful, we needed to learn how to read data and analyze information on demographics from places such as Google Analytics. Analytics help measure the effectiveness of your marketing strategies and allow you to make better informed decisions. Track your metrics for website traffic, social media engagement and email open rates.

You can easily do this on most social media platforms.

If you aren't measuring these activities, you are throwing your money away and simply guessing about what your spent dollars are actually buying!

Don't spend one dollar unless you can track what it will do for you! At the same time, don't be afraid to experiment to see what works best!

Email Marketing

Emails are gold! If you can obtain an email from a person, now you have a free pathway to market directly to them! However, don't abuse the relationship! Make sure you create and use emails with integrity.

The upside of emails is this: Once you have a person's email address, there are no more costs!

If you gain access to someone's inbox, you have a portal into their world. Once you motivate someone to read your email, you can inform them, support them, challenge them and possibly turn them into clients.

Use your donor email list to keep in touch with them regularly. Send them newsletters, invitations and thank you responses for supporting your organization. Emails enable easier sharing of progress stories and articulating specific needs to more easily encourage donations and increase volunteerism. Emails are also the least expensive way to market. Compared to advertising, social media purchases and in person events, there is little or no cost for emails.

What to Avoid:

Sending out meaningless emails

Thinking of only what you want

Overwhelming the person with dribble

Wasting their time

What to Do:

Become an expert in this area! Yes, you can be an expert in any area by using YouTube. YouTube contains a vast array of free information from companies who want you to be a client of theirs. Pay attention to the details in their messages. Study the various parts of their messages and pay particular attention to identifying key parts often referred to as a "header," the "body" of their message, the sales pitch or "ask" as well as a send-off or "salutation."

Track emails you send and note which responses are most positive. Count these as "conversions." If you are able to afford one, use a Customer Relationship Management (CRM) system to help manage and analyze customer interactions and data throughout the customer lifecycle for this function.

Find a way to capture emails.

Remember this is a free lead. Even though it's free, treat it like gold. If you want to have people open the emails you send out, make sure your emails provide value in the form of needed information and a respectful message. Ideally you want your stakeholders to read the emails you send them and feel good and thankful for receiving it.

Email Marketing

Despite the proliferation of social media, email remains a powerful tool for nonprofit marketing. It's best used for direct communication with supporters to share updates, solicit donations and nurture established relationships. Email campaigns can be personalized and segmented for different groups within your audience base. This flexibility makes them a highly effective tool to reach out to potential donors, volunteers and advocates.

Co-Branding

Partner with Local Businesses: Collaborating with local businesses by asking them to sponsor an event with you. They can either underwrite the event, share the costs or invite their clients to meet more people who support your organization. By jointly sponsoring events, your organization and the co-branding partner business can each increase visibility as well as credibility. It's a win-win situation where businesses are able to demonstrate corporate as well as social responsibility while nonprofits gain access to broader audiences.

Tell a story about your Agency!

Utilize Storytelling: People connect with stories more than statistics. Sharing impactful stories of the people or causes the nonprofit supports can be a powerful way to engage and motivate people.

Things to Do:

1. Understand your audience! Be aware of your target audience and cater to their needs, preferences and how they prefer receiving information. Tailor your message to your audience. This is crucial for engagement.
2. Plan and execute targeted fundraising campaigns. Effective campaigns are often story-driven, making a direct connection between the donor's contribution and the impact it will have.
3. Having a compelling mission as well as the content and the right visuals will help you.
4. Attend community events and host your own. Participating in community events, conferences and workshops go a long way to develop public awareness. Hosting events — even virtual ones — is another great way to engage the community.

Clear Branding and Messaging:

Who is your target market? It is important to establish a strong, clear brand identity with messaging designed to resonate with your target audience. The words you use, the impressions you make and the optics which include pictures or graphics will help the people and groups with whom you want to partner to know you better.

Three things you should accomplish in every marketing experience.

Motivate people to:

- Know you
- Like you
- Trust you

Whenever you're making contact with a donor or creating a presentation for public use, the following questions will provide the appropriate perspective. Ask these questions in all things public and in your customer service:

Does this allow people to know us better?

Will this make the public like us?

Will the public trust us when they see what we are doing?

A significant way people learn to trust you is transparency. Report the activities in which your organization is involved. Doing this on a regular basis is impactful, informative and will build a base more receptive to your messages. Doing this regularly will also create a larger pool of volunteers to help you with activities, events and whenever you seek donations. Transparency builds trust and credibility with your supporters.

Network and Collaborate:

Too often, nonprofits become silos with no entry points in which to establish relationships with other agencies. Many lack the resolve to reach out to others. However, my experience shows building relationships with other nonprofits, community leaders and influencers will open doors to new opportunities and additional resources.

Do these things to create a larger community:

- Join the local chamber of commerce.
- Go to conferences and reach out to several people from your community and beyond.
- Invite members of the city council to have coffee with you and provide them with a presentation of what you do.
- Join a local or state association to represent your interests.
- Form partnerships and collaborations.
- Engage other organizations, businesses or influencers to expand your reach and resources.

It is always encouraging when nonprofits decide to go after a grant together. Keep their individual missions separate, yet partner with others seeking resources which will grow both agencies. Doing this will bring more revenue and create brighter futures for both organizations.

Volunteer Engagement:

Engaging volunteers not only helps in achieving more with less, it also turns volunteers into ambassadors for a cause. Encourage and enable your supporters and volunteers to become advocates for your cause, spreading the word within their respective networks.

SCALING UP!

How and when should a leader decide to scale up their nonprofit? It all depends on where you want to take your organization. Based on what you know now, where would you like your organization to be next year? In three years? Next decade? Having an idea of who you want your organization to serve and who you are serving will help you determine how big your footprint must be. Asking this question often will help you clarify the decisions you need to make daily.

How fast do you desire to grow? This often depends on how large you want your organization to be. Answering this question will give you a good idea of how much time you need to meet your expectations.

I find this process a little more difficult than what motivational books present when they say you should multiply by 10 times everything you do.

It makes more sense to me to evaluate the services you do now. For framework, then look at others in your genre, industry or those organization who offer services similar to yours. Ask yourself if there are other organizations you believe are on a similar track. By doing this, you can see what direction you might want to take in order to grow your organization. Others might have already discovered funding for things you are interested in doing. While you, like me, don't want to compete, it is an excellent strategy to see who in your area of interest is doing things well and has figured things out.

Once you have decided which new services you want to expand or what services you would like to add, then you can begin to determine at what pace you want your organization to grow.

Much of what we do in the beginning is guess about how large we want our services to be.

I have grown organizations from a first-year revenue of under $50,000 to eventually more than $15 million per year.

This is a solid way to design your strategy. However, in all transparency, I have a much simpler way of growing an organization. First, I look at the total number of people in need of my organization's services.

Second, I examine what other agencies are providing the same or similar services.

Next, my team and I design our services to exemplify the best possible way to serve our potential clients.

Finally, we set up systems and processes to identify future clients and decide how we will onboard these new clients. This will include seeing life through their eyes and continually listening to our clients, employees and administration's input as we roll out these services.

A concept I use is to calculate how long it will take to double the size of important things like investments and growth of an organization.

The Law of 72

If you want to double the size of your organization, use the Law of 72. This guide states if want to double your size in three years, divide 3 years into 72 parts and this will determine you should grow at a compound rate of 20 percent annually in order to double in size within three years.

Benefits of Scaling up!

The benefits of scaling up your organization are numerous. However, so are the complications. Thinking about the future for most Executive Directors (EDs) includes establishing a growth rate. Most leaders do not want to continue at the same rate of growth.

Most EDs feel a responsibility to grow the organization more rapidly!

Growth can affect your organization by creating reserves for use in pivoting. In turn, these reserves will enable you to meet demands you cannot foresee from where you are currently. Growth also creates its own energy and belief in the future for you and your entire team.

The perception of your organization will become one of a well managed and dynamic organization. The community you serve will quickly realize you want to serve more of their needs than already exist in the community. Also, funders will quickly learn your organization will require and, more importantly, successfully manage larger amounts of funding.

Every funder I know looks for the healthiest and most creative organizations to support financially. Also, they realize your organization can correctly process large amounts of funds and quickly scale up when new needs arise.

Unfortunately, many nonprofit organizations don't grow or refuse to scale up?

These are the organizations which will not have substantial enough reserves to grow or even weather tough situations. Cash flow may become a problem for such organizations. These organizations may not use or be able to acquire necessary technology to assist them in complicated situations. Talented employees are more likely to leave these organizations because competing agencies which are growing will likely pay more. The organization's future may soon look too bleak to attract top talent! Due to a lack of resources, the organization's culture could be thrown into chaos more often. The reserves organizations require for fast pivots and flexibility may no longer exist.

Reasons to Scale Up:

You may need or want new processes, systems and tools to make your organization more efficient. Scaling up gives an organization extra dollars to take advantage of technology or consulting. Scaling up provides an opportunity to streamline operations, which also may help reduce costs. Scaling up also allows expansion geographically to places where more services can be provided, thus bringing in additional revenue and usually higher margins.

Benefits of Scaling Up:

Scaling up usually provides an economy of scale. It also allows you to afford a Corporate Financial Officer (CFO), Human Resource (HR) professionals or other resources to expand your accounting department. When organizations scale up, they usually spread operational costs across more service sectors, thus lowering per capita costs. Having better talent to work with also allows you to become stronger and healthier, ensuring a better future for the organization.

Scaling up increases the resilience of organizations. If an organization can develop multiple revenue streams or divisions, a single division within the organization may not be doing well in one season while a different division might be expanding in such a way it is able to provide enough financial growth to keep the entire organization stable.

Skills Necessary for Scaling Up:

The long-term horizon approach uncovers those skills your organization will need for the future. If you are thinking about scaling up an organization, you may require skills relating to project management or budgeting so you can more accurately project costs and tabulate revenues. You may also want to become more familiar with spreadsheets as an organizational leadership skill.

If you are going to grow your agency, think about the impact on your position within the organization and what additional skills you require to effectively lead the larger and more complex organization.

When our organization moved from $1 Million in revenues to $4 Million, we needed better planning. We completed a thorough realignment of duties and, where necessary, identified leaders to head each of the resulting new divisions. Requirements of scaling up may force you to include people who have more specialized skills. This may include a CFO if you grow beyond $10 Million to $15 million.

What other types of people and skill sets will you need to complement your own skills?

You most likely will want to hire people who have skills you don't personally possess. This is the only way to cover all your bases while creating a stronger leadership team.

Scaling up will also likely demand you to learn skills in supervising satellite sites while holding people at each work site accountable for results when you aren't physically present. It will also require a leadership team capable of recruiting and training new leaders and skills in supervision of remote leaders.

During your scaling up process, you'll also need to maintain the same high quality of services and job performance which allowed you to expand. Growth rarely comes unless you have excelled in one area or have a strength other organizations don't possess. Maintaining a key competitive advantage is associated with the quality of services you provide. Focusing on quality remains imperative even as your organization grows.

Use Incentives to Grow Faster!

Providing incentives to key people is usually wise when growing an organization.

During my years of leading nonprofit organizations, I witnessed the immense value of incentives. Incentives allowed me to increase wages of valued employees when the organization was growing, especially when I noticed these same individuals were also growing their own capabilities and responsibilities.

Incentives are a powerful form of energy for expanding your organization. It is necessary, therefore, to weigh the pros and cons of using additional benefits to reward certain positions.

Incentives Inspire People!

> *"If you want to predict how people will behave,*
> *you just have to look at their incentives."*

Charlie Munger

Munger believed incentives drive behavior and outcomes. Understanding what motivates people is crucial for predicting their actions.

You can predictably retain top talent when you judiciously use incentives. This allows the organization's goals for growth to be accomplished more quickly. Incentives can also be a tool when encouraging employees to act and think like owners. This often will result in employees putting in more energy, solving problems faster and taking more pride in their individual accomplishments. Employees will enjoy building a larger organization and serving more people if they are also rewarded.

> *"Show me the incentive and I will show you the outcome."*

Charlie Munger

My point of view on this subject: When an organization grows through the efforts of other employees, why shouldn't they be rewarded?

Why should I spend my time motivating others when they can be motivated by incentives to solve problems and accomplish the organizition's goals.

Incentives are a powerful driver of the creation of systems to create great outcomes. When employing incentives, new systems are naturally put into place to monitor employees and ensure agreed-upon results are achieved. There is real power in these systems. When growth occurs, money is generally tight, so I use incentives to get better outcomes by motivating higher quality while also improving efficiencies. Use incentives for what you want to see.

What future results do you want to see?

Here are some quotes on the topic of using incentives to produce better results and outcomes:

"Be clear about what you want
and reward the behaviors that produce it."

Les Schwab

"No man will make a great leader
who wants to do it all himself
or get all the credit for doing it."

Andrew Carnegie

This highlights the importance of motivating others by distributing responsibility and giving them the opportunity to succeed, which can act as a powerful incentive.

"What gets measured gets managed."

Peter Drucker

This quote implies measurement and rewards tied to performance metrics can drive better outcomes. In short, what you pay for, in most cases, is the monitoring of a system you have created and desire to see it work in the way it was designed.

When you implement an incentive, there are two things you are trying to accomplish.

First, motivate your people.

Second, maintain high standards to bring about the behavior or actions you desire.

For incentives to work, you also need the following:

Clear Goals

The goals must be clear and the outcome communicated. The goals also must be measurable. Whoever is receiving the incentive needs to know what is expected of their efforts. The reason to use incentives is to bring about changes desired in the organization. Even broader, you desire results to be accomplished with a minimal amount of effort.

Relevance

Are the incentives being used to make something happen or maintain a standard relevant to the organization's needs?

Timeliness

Be timely in granting the incentive. The recipient should know exactly when it is coming. They also should know why they are receiving the incentive. Correct timeliness should bring about the behavior you desire or the task completed when required.

The impact:

Immediate rewards reinforce desired behavior more effectively than delayed incentives.

Consistency

Being consistent with incentives is an important part of the incentive process.

What I find necessary is to check with the employee and determine whether they are in fact receiving the incentive raise as promised. Sometimes there may be a glitch in accounting, or the person forgets to apply for the incentive pay.

Combine systems and incentives

One of the most powerful ways to have incentives work is to combine them with new systems also being implemented. I used an incentive when I reduced a billing office from three employees down to two. We were experiencing nothing but trouble from our billing office. Files were out of compliance and there was regular drama. This caused low morale.

I talked the situation over with my leadership team. We discovered we could do the job with just two employees because we needed better results, lower drama and higher quality in terms of customer service.

Therefore, we incentivized three areas of the billing process which would be paid out on a monthly basis if our requirements were met.

When audited by the clinical director on a monthly basis, 90 percent of the files generated would be perfect with zero errors.

The two employees would each receive an incentive if all the billing and paperwork required by our funders received no "claw backs." In the past, our funders refused to pay us if they found errors in our billing. This was called a "claw back."

All receivables from each billing cycle needed to be less than 60 days old.

Once they accomplished each condition, the incentive was paid.

How many times do you think I needed to address problems in the incentivized areas?

The answer: Never! Incentives well placed and thought through pressures those doing the work, not upon you or any other direct supervisor.

Align Incentives with System Goals

When systems are aligned with goals, you often achieve better efficiency, higher quality and greater satisfaction from customers as well as staff.

I also use incentives in cyber security. We desired to reduce the potential for cyber blackmail where someone is able to take over a computer server and lock us out. At the time, companies were frequently held hostage to obtain access to their vital information and would pay ransom ranging from hundreds of thousands to many millions of dollars.

We called on some experts who were selling cyber security services and listened to their sales pitch. They all offered great systems for our protection, however they would typically cost us more than $10,000 per month. When extrapolated out 10 years, we realized we would be paying more than $1 Million for this so-called protection. This proposed payment amount was untenable to us.

A few days after we heard their sales presentation, our management team gathered again. Some of my staffers wanted to go with a security company. I was firmly against any such agreement. Some of our newest employees were unused to thinking outside the box. Therefore, we began to brainstorm how we could achieve more security for far lower cost. We came up with three requirements.

We needed to create a security system for a total cost of no more than $10,000.

We desired to lose no more than one week's data if we were ever attacked or hijacked.

We agreed to monitor our security system on a weekly basis.

My staff and I came up with a plan we've used for more than four years and we've enhanced the original system as well as how staff monitors the system and handles replacement of an external hard drive every week in order to receive a financial incentive. By being clear about our goals, we refused to be trapped in a system costing 10 times or more annually without giving us any more security.

To be effective, incentives should have the following elements and impact more than one area:

Outcome-Based Metrics:

Use clear, objective metrics within the system and linked to incentives.

Ensure transparency and fairness so people understand how their performance will be evaluated and rewarded.

Equitable access to rewards is achieved when everyone working within the system has a fair opportunity to achieve the incentives offered.

Adjust incentives based on system performance If the system is underperforming or hitting bottlenecks, incentives might need to restructuring.

Incentivize process improvement by building into the system any incentives for creating ways to improve the system itself.

When not to use incentives!

As soon as people stop caring about the cause and simply work for added money, not because they truly desire to help.

When donors get upset. People who give money may think it wasteful to offer incentives or bonuses instead of helping people.

If incentives cause issues, review your process and outcome to see how you can resolve the new issues.

It's hard to be fair. Figure out who truly deserves an incentive or bonus as some people might feel cheated if their efforts are not noticed or rewarded.

When participating staffers start doing just the easy stuff, not the important stuff. Keep their focus on those things the nonprofit truly needs.

THE ULTIMATE QUESTION

I was getting ready to address a national conference at McCormick Place in Chicago. One of my faults is I often pick up a new book and get so interested in its content I attempt to include this in my presentation. My friend Jack was with me on this trip and kept me focused on my presentation. However, it usually requires a powerful intervention to move me out of a quest to find additional information to cram into a presentation. Well, I eventually gave in to Jack's hounding and refocused on my existing presentation.

Nevertheless, the book I picked up transformed the way I see customer service and how to assess customer satisfaction. The book is **The Ultimate Question** by Fred Reichheld. Since I first read it many years ago, the book was updated in 2011 as **The Ultimate Question 2.0 (Revised and Expanded Edition): How Net Promoter Companies Thrive in a Customer-Driven World,** co-authored by Fred Reichheld and Rob Markey. The book focuses on the concept of customer loyalty as a key indicator of a company's future success.

The ultimate question referred to in the book's title is this: "How likely is it for you to recommend our company, product or service to a friend or colleague?"

Survey responses were then categorized as Promoters, Passives or Detractors and evaluated in such a way to determine a Net Promoter Score (NPS) or a Net Promoter System (NPS), a customer-centric management framework explained in the book. The broader NPS system incorporates business processes to improve customer experience and drive profitable growth.

Reichheld argues in the book, companies with higher NPS scores tend to grow faster and be more successful because they focus on creating high-quality experiences to foster customer loyalty. His book emphasizes genuine, sustainable growth which comes from having customers who love your products or services enough to recommend them to others.

In essence, The Ultimate Question 2.0 advocates focusing on the needs of the customer. The main goal is not merely to satisfy customers, but to delight them to a point they become advocates for your brand.

Reichheld thesis is that customer loyalty and delight is a more reliable predictor of company growth than traditional customer satisfaction surveys. He also believes using a single metric is better than most of the satisfaction surveys organizations typically send out. For those who like to measure things, Reichheld developed a Net Promoter Score to measure customer loyalty and satisfaction.

> *"There is only one way to grow a business profitably.*
> *Make sure your customers are treated so well*
> *they come back for more and bring their friends."*

Fred Reichheld

I like his approach because he narrows it down to a single question to determine both loyalty and satisfaction on the part of customers. This, therefore, is the Ultimate Question:

"Would you recommend our services to a friend or relative?"

Responses to this important question tell leaders so much about their organization. It provides an indication of whether people support what you do. Not only that, if you dig a little deeper, you can also determine an organization's strengths. It also allows leaders to find out more about their clients, such as: "What specifically impresses and pleases people."

This is important to know. Why? Because you can often enhance services or do more of whatever is working.

If you have the courage to ask this question and get a "No, I wouldn't refer my friends or family," you are now in a much stronger position to want to make your organization better.

Why?

Because this person was likely offended or disrespected or experienced a less than satisfactory experience and their response indicates this. Conversely, there may be something going on in your organization in need of immediate attention. You may have systemic problems which annoy or upset clients.

*"Employees must be able to treat customers and colleagues
alike in such a manner it makes all of them proud."*

Fred Reichheld

On the other hand, this response can be seen as an amazing gift!

What gift, you might ask. Well, you discover some great information and make changes to become the great organization you want to be. Don't categorize it as a rare bad experience and doubt the feedback's validity. If you do, you may not realize how often such a bad experience happens.

RESPOND TO CRITICISM

Criticism is one of the hardest things to take. Especially when you work at the highest level you know how and are concerned about serving your clients and other stakeholders. However, criticism often walks hand in hand with leadership.

When I started my first nonprofit, I was treating heroin addicts. We were a Christian organization providing services without regard to the ability of a client to pay for our services. Most of our clients' families wanted nothing more to do with them. Our clients burned all their bridges as a result of their addiction and no one they knew would even give them a quarter when asked.

My agency relied on volunteers. In fact, for a long time I was the only paid employee.

One of my volunteers was an older gentleman who was in recovery from a similar addiction problem. Since we required all of our volunteers to remain sober and not under the influence, this person would remain awake all night and ensure our clients were complying with the rules and everyone was safe.

Eventually, however, I heard a rumor this volunteer relapsed and was using drugs again. It was my job to hold a conversation with him to find out the circumstances.

Having a volunteer with a responsible position in a treatment center who is accused of using is often a death blow to a program as it often causes clients to walk out of a program or start using while in treatment and ultimately die.

I talked to the gentleman and made a decision to release him from his position.

One month later, the man died. Almost immediately, one of our former clients started telling everyone I was the cause of the gentleman's death.

I reacted and started building a case for my defense. Fortunately, I received excellent counsel from a pastor friend who said, "Leaders get accused falsely at times and the best thing to do is to state the truth and let it go."

I followed his advice and almost as quickly as the rumor-driven firestorm started, it extinguished itself. People made up their minds about what was true and what wasn't. Then, we all moved on.

Two former clients who probably didn't like me anyway became distant from our program. Most everybody else saw my point of view or expressed compassion on this man and his family's situation.

What to do When Mistakes are Made

No matter how hard you try, mistakes will be made. Similarly, when leaders make a decision, sometimes things will go against what the leader intended.

A good leader realizes it is impossible to be perfect. In order to stop disappointing yourself or other people, the best thing a leader can do is admit the error to those it matters to and act differently next time around.

Wisdom comes from either studying how to do things correctly or a combination of study and making mistakes you regret. If you do reflect on the regrettable, do so in such a way it bring you to a depth of wisdom you previously didn't have.

CONSISTENCY IS KEY

The value of being consistent cannot be underestimated! Almost every great undertaking is brought about because someone was consistent. Whether it be Picasso or Tom Brady, they both were consistent at what they did and they mastered their craft because of their consistency. This concept was brought home to me in its simplicity when I heard a nutritionist speak. I have always had a struggle with an extra 20 pounds I wanted to shed permanently.

The nutritionist suggested the idea of diets is a false method. He said it is better to decide what you like to eat, make sure it is healthy, then consistently eat those foods. I like this idea. Why eat something you have no desire to ever eat again as soon as you hit a certain weight. It changed how I ate from that point on.

How does this apply to leadership? Well, being consistent with your people creates trust. Being consistent with how you handle your organization's finances can help keep you solid financially. Being consistent in reading and studying year after year will make you a great leader. Consistently reviewing your goals will help you obtain them. **Consistency matters more than any other thing you do.**

I found this out with my grandchildren. I have a grandson who likes to spend time with me. I once asked him what he would like to do when we are together.

"Papa, you like to eat weird foods and so do I. Why don't we eat interesting foods together," he responded.

I took this to heart and every month we try out a new restaurant and eat a new cuisine. We research the country where the cuisine originated while we are eating. We then discuss how the food is prepared and what makes it unique. This consistent activity brings us closer together as he and I grow older.

Consistency is akin to habits. One of my favorite authors in the area of habits is James Clear.

"Every action you take is a vote for the person you wish to become."

James Clear – Atomic Actions

A NONPROFIT LEADER'S EDGE

"The doers are the major thinkers.
The people that really create the things that change this industry
are both the thinker and doer in the same person."

Steve Jobs

In my opinion, consistent action is the sign of a great leader.

I was mentoring a coach of a girl's high school soccer team. We were implementing character development as well as teaching soccer skills. We observed many of these young athletes were affected by self-talk. Whenever one of the girls made a mistake on the field, she would stop for a fraction of a second and reflect on her mistake. The opposing team took note of this behavioral quirk and began to take advantage of our team by making moves to place our team at a disadvantage on the soccer field.

As leaders, we sometimes do the same thing. Leaders usually work within a longer time frame, however, when we are moving forward on a project. Eventually, something eventually goes array and we may back away or even lose forward momentum.

It is important to act consistently. You may need to take a breather for a moment. However, it is important you continue to move forward.

Our leadership team decided to enhance how we were providing services. We decided to participate in a contract competition in a county where we were the newbies. We decided we were going to participate at a higher level than our competition. The upside; it would affect us in a positive way financially. We were underfunded for years and this change in attitude to enhance how we provided services to our clients quickly became a game changer for us.

To make sure we retained a competitive advantage, I decided to hire the best consultant in the nation. We offered to pay between $5,000 to 15,000 for the consultant's services.

When my team expressed high hopes to land the desired contract, I reflected on what they said. Interestingly, this didn't matter to me since I wanted to participate regardless of the result. However, I was excited about the information delivered by the consultant. The experience of participating also served us well going forward. We acquired more knowledge in a shorter period of time than we could ever obtain in any other way because we were attempting to play at a much higher level. These two factors gave me encouragement for the future.

Nothing replaces knowledge, action and experience. By competing and raising our game, we were able to acquire all three.

THE IMPORTANCE OF SYSTEMS

*"You do not rise to the level of your goals,
you fall to the level of your systems."*

James Clear

*"Goals do not determine success,
systems determine success!"*

James Clear

Systems are what it takes to lead people to accomplish results and maintain high standards. Standards plus systems are unequalled in creating top performance! I will deal with standards in the next chapter. First, we need to better understand how systems work.

To find what systems you need to design first, ask yourself this:

What are three things in need of change in our organization today?

When I launched my first nonprofit, I began with just $14,000 to invest in the venture. Let me tell you, having some cash on hand is comforting. However, it also meant I needed to get busy creating results or my cash money would disappear in three or four months. My twin boys were just 13 at the time, yet they knew how to work. Jeff and Jason helped me clean up the new office and get it painted. It was amazing to see how much effort they gave me in those early days.

We did everything on the cheap. I couldn't afford any administrative help, so I took on every job: accountant, transporter, social worker, lice remover, janitor, marketer, etc.

My point? I was desperate, so I needed to quickly bring in as much revenue as possible while doing a great job at all of the other tasks simultaneously.

When you start out, you are usually in survival mode. At times, I wondered whether I would make it. Would I quit what I was doing and take a different job? Or do I admit defeat because I ran out of money and simply go to work for someone else?

From the start, we developed systems to identify our organization as something different. It was a real turning point for us. We implemented many systems enabling us to say, "This is what makes us different."

What have I learned from all this? The systems we implemented allowed me to have more free time to work on improving our agency. This is how we were able to grow from a personal loan of $14,000 into an organization with revenues exceeding $15 million annually.

I no longer wanted to be the only person with all the answers because then I would be required to single-handedly address every question or fix every problem. I wanted to have a smooth operation where almost everything was thought out ahead of time and our people knew what to do and what was expected of them, even in a crisis.

Now, let me be transparent. I do have control tendencies. I love a good adrenaline rush as much as anyone.

My first professional job after the military and leaving college was running a drug and alcohol treatment program. I worked seven days a week, from early morning to 10 p.m. or later each night. I loved all the activity and I was central to every crisis needing resolution. However, this work schedule is only possible when you are in your late 20s or early 30s because it certainly was not good for my sanity, health or personal relationships.

This is why systems, protocols and "our way of doing things" are important to me. I want to see our organization be able to function without me.

The most valuable thing I can do as a leader is to think! Spending most of my work time involved with every detail of running an organization does not allow me time to make the important decisions or think through the next steps towards growth as I continue to develop a company capable of transforming lives; not only the lives of our clients and their foster parents, but the lives of our employees and volunteers as well.

I also learned to put most of my energy into working on the organization and less time working in it. I learned this lesson only after 10 years running my nonprofit. At the time of my epiphany, I was responsible for 10 employees. Yet, I continued to be the only person who could assess foster care placements, coordinate which homes the children went into and do all the logistics of meeting with a county worker and arranging the child to be picked up or deliver the child where they were supposed to go.

I clearly remember the night when I finally said, enough is enough!

It was 2012, I was navigating Interstate 5 in northern California heading home after working all day. My pager suddenly went off. This was well before texting became the great communications tool it is today. I glanced at the pager's display of the caller's phone number and realized it was from a county social worker. I immediately pulled over to the road's edge and called the social worker. Her message: the county needed an emergency placement for two young children. I then scoured my list of families who would be appropriate for this placement and proceeded to make several phone calls. Eventually, the foster parents returned my call to let me know they could take care of these two young children. I then called the social worker back and we arranged how to transport the children to their new foster home. All of this transpired in a bit more than 45 minutes late at night while parked along a dark and foreboding freeway.

By the time I resumed my trip and safely returned home, I began to think about training my other employees to do what I was doing out there on the side of a freeway late at night.

I reflected on why I hadn't yet included others in the placement of children. Was I afraid they would find the child an inappropriate placement? Was I concerned the county would be upset at us for not handling things correctly? Did I think my staff was incapable of doing this function correctly?

As you might imagine, all those concerns were important to me. What was more concerning, however, was how much I was involved in every aspect of what we did on a regular basis. Imagine what might happen if I just kept taking on more and more duties as we grew as an agency? Most concerning was how I was invalidating an important precept of mine to develop and grow my staff. How could they truly develop ownership and grow if I was not allowing them to learn more about the logistical end of our services? How long would my staff stay with our organization if they ceased to be challenged?

At this realization, I decided to train my top people to do one of the most important administrative tasks of a foster care agency, the placement of children into foster homes.

Shortly after this realization, I quit doing placements. I haven't personally been responsible for placing another child for more than 13 years. Even my new staff does a much better job than I was doing because we have very clear systems for each placement.

Because we needed to change, the knowledge I acquired needed to be shared with all our people.

We then started to put our system down in writing: "How we place children."

We wrote down what the process was and how we would maintain our standards of care. We did this the way we always create systems by beginning with the end result in mind. This is how we created one of our most impactful systems. We follow these systems and standards to make sure everyone is doing the same thing.

The point is, once you find a best practice, standardize it. Train employees to make sure everyone knows the best practice and follows it to the letter. Leaders are the keepers of the standards and systems. If you have an excellent system backed up by solid standards, do not let anyone violate it or your quality will certainly deteriorate.

Embarrassingly, most of the systems we created came about because someone was frustrated or upset when we or they missed our desired target of excellence.

How to create a system:

I understand most people find little interest in the concept of creating systems. However, I get excited every time we implement a new system within our organization.

Why do I think this way?

I believe systems do some amazing things for our organizations. In fact, if you are not already operating with this perspective, I predict you will eventually encounter more than your share of drama, personnel issues and the accompanying drop in production in certain areas. Not relying on systems may mean that you may be in a personality driven organization.

An example of not using a system of improvement reminds me of this experience involving a friend of mine. When my friend was a child, he showed enormous talent as a musician. However, as he aged, he simply relied on natural skill and capacity. He never learned the lessons others suffered through just to be invited to join the band. He never really challenged himself to be at the next level, which meant he didn't learn how to grind or take himself to a higher level. Consequently, when he hit his late 20s, other musicians who did the hard work to improve their level of mastery easily passed him up. My friend never developed the positive habits around learning and practice. Therefore, he didn't have the grit to persevere when he encountered barriers. Developing a system of excellence, whether for inherently gifted leaders or those who have more challenges, takes people to the highest level at which they can comfortably perform. Systems are the foundation for developing great athletes, performers and, most of all, great leaders and coaches!

I once believed I held a successful problem-solving meeting with a group of employees only to find out two months after we agreed on specific changes needed, those ideas were never implemented by any of those employees. As time passed, they simply went back to doing things the same old way.

This experience told me that just talking is usually an ineffective leadership style. A leader who spends a lot of time talking will produce very little in terms of results. Accountability needs to be a part of system development. For leaders, this means we need to have a plan and check back to ensure it is being implemented so others can evaluate results of the new system.

To determine if a problem needs a system solution, leaders should ask these questions:

- How often does this happen?
- Why does this happen?
- What needs to be done to keep it from happening again?
- How do we devise a solution?
- Was everyone concerned allowed to weigh in with their suggestions?

Very often, people with little experience in the trenches as a leader in the corporate or nonprofit world won't place much value in systems.

Even the most experienced leaders including accountants, senior leaders and even CEOs isolated from work-a-day issues don't seem to have a clue how powerful systems can be for fixing problems and ensuring they stay fixed.

I am a firm believer in systems for the following reasons:

They eliminate strife and personnel issues. Most of all, they help us operate at peak efficiency and get results faster. The best organizations rely on systems! Without systems, the focus is usually on what's not working. This usually turns a problem area into personal issues which brings confrontation, blame, scapegoating or worse.

Systems can support best practices as well as optimum standards so your organization can operate at a higher level than it ever has in the past. Systems can eliminate unnecessary work and often eliminate extra personnel. I have eliminated 30 percent of labor on projects just by analyzing problems and the mistakes being made.

Systems help you simplify the complex and create norms in your organizations. This allows everyone to know what to do in order to achieve a desired result. Consistency comes from having reliable systems because they raise expectations of how things should operate.

I'll give you an example of how systems work for our organization. We offer a counseling program with a billing office staffed by three people. Since the program began, I continually noticed we were experiencing low productivity. Our paperwork wasn't filed correctly and there was always paper stacked around the office. More than once, my people were becoming upset with each other. I reflected on what my own expectations were for this program. I realized my people were trusted hard-working individuals who were with me for a long time. Therefore, I took on the responsibility for fixing the problem.

Defining the problem and figuring out what needed to be fixed was my first priority. This is not an easy task when the only feedback received was complaints. In order to find out the information I needed before I implemented solutions, I used a coaching approach to ask each employee what they individually saw as the problem. I also asked each person what he or she would do differently if they were in charge.

After listening to their complaints, I received conformation of my own observations. Furthermore, I received feedback about a lack of space for tools including computers and printers. However, the greatest complaint was the animosity between employees. Interestingly, during this process one of the three employees quit. This presented a more immediate problem. As I thought of a possible solution, new questions bubbled up.

Could we run the billing office with two employees instead of three?

Since my employees knew more about this area than I did, I let them tell me what needed improvement. Also, I didn't want to hire another employee and see the same old issues crop up again. After some personal reflection, I asked the director of the division and another trusted employee in the same department to share their ideas of what to include in a workable solution. During this conversation I asked whether we could function with only two employees versus the three employees we previously assigned. Surprisingly, they thought it would be worth a try to keep the billing office staffed with two employees because of the strife three employees seemed to bring.

I decided to incentivize three areas. At first, the two staffers were upset at the idea of being incentivized. However, as they rapidly grew to master various requirements, they earned more money whenever they met their goals. I could pay them more because eliminating one employee meant the incentives came from lower net operating costs.

The results were spectacular. Accuracy and documentation each improved. The paperwork and files looked better than ever and we were able to catch errors before the auditors saw them, which meant we didn't lose any more money!

Improving the system boiled down to fixing three things we needed to increase production, culture and services for our clinicians. Because they worked with a system designed to meet our standards, the two employees maintained the process and would grumble and complain only when anyone violated the new system's guidelines.

When you have a great system and someone violates it or allows standards to slide, there is a gnashing of teeth and people generally become disagreeable with the culprit.

We discovered two employees were more than adequate to handle the billing office. This system started many years ago. Except for a few tweaks shortly after it began, it is as reliable as clockwork.

One unintended consequence of the new system, our therapists soon began to rely on the billing staff's help in maintaining their charts at such a high level.

How do you know you need a new system or revitalize an old one?

This is a great question! Very few people come up to me and say, "We need a new system." They usually come to me or I find out by going to them to discuss any difficulties when I ask how things are going. At those times, they usually complain or express frustration with several things not working as smoothly as they believe it should. I generally use the following questions to get to the truth in the situation:

- Why isn't the system working? Is it because it is not being used or has it become inadequate for our needs?
- If you were in charge, what would you do?
- What is the problem? Can you define it in one sentence?
- What should people do differently?
- What is your plan to fix this situation?
- Why wasn't this problem solved? What solutions have you tried?
- What or who is the key obstacle to solving this problem?

Problems are usually presented to leaders in the form of a complaint or whining. Other leaders sometimes describe their employees to me in this manner: "They're just whining."

I cringe whenever I hear this because these leaders are dismissing very real concerns of their employees. I don't ever use the word whining to describe a person who is making their case to me because it is offensive. I see this information as valuable as it often pinpoints some very valid concerns. When people talk to leaders, it is imperative to discern the motivation behind the complaint.

In system development, I'm not talking about following the whims of chronic complainers. I'm referring to real issues presented by quality people with whom I need to pay attention.

You won't always get the truth from the people you interview about a problem. What you'll get usually are some complaints and a point of view where the complainer sounds like a victim.

My observation is most people aren't used to solving problems. They also aren't accustomed to creating systems. In most conversations, language concerning change actually prevents progress. These conversations usually begin with, "I didn't want to hurt any feelings, so I didn't bring it up."

We live in a culture which typically avoids straight conversations because of cowardice or at the very least, a belief that honesty is rude. People will make comments about their co-workers and talk only when the subject person is not present. However, they will do almost anything to avoid an uncomfortable conversation with a co-worker.

The following reasons are why we tend to avoid uncomfortable conversations. These are also the reasons most organizations are not operating in a healthy manner and rapidly become toxic work environments:

- Whether paid employees or volunteer, our people have never been required to have adult conversations.
- People are used to blaming and not solving problems.
- One person exhibits a strong personality and others are afraid of being straight with him or her.
- They expect leadership to solve all problems.
- They may not value good systems or understand their power.

Not having adult conversations or confrontations with others is, in my opinion, the major cause of most personnel problems. Sometimes leaders will not do their job to confront situations because they think people won't like them or there will be a rebellion.

My experience is just the opposite. Almost every time I initiate an adult conversation regarding a confrontation, people are receptive. However, doing this takes real courage!

If any of my leaders or I are silently wondering, "Wouldn't you think they would know better?"during a meeting, this reaction is a clear indication my team and I are not taking responsibility for the problem. We are giving our power away and beginning to act like victims.

Here's why. If someone is not doing necessary tasks or completing them in an inefficient manner, you may be the one who must change.

Employees who continually mess up either lack training or were never held accountable for their own lack of production or poor attitude. Accountability is part of the delegation process. However, delegating is only a small part of the solution. The other part is following up to make sure the assignment is being addressed and done correctly within a requested time frame.

Sometimes leaders are negligent because a conversation with a person messing up did not include questions about their own perspective regarding the issue.

Creating a system:

To create a system, first you need to find what is not working. This may be people in conflict and blaming each other or discovering someone who has taken on too much work and is therefore overwhelmed and not completing all of their tasks satisfactorily.

One of my habits is to walk around a work site so I can visit with my staff and observe any obstacles preventing or hampering them from doing their best work. Almost always, when I show interest in what they are doing and ask, "What's on your plate?" or "What's on your mind in relation to what you are doing at work?" I generally receive a response regarding some difficulty such as they are waiting on delivery of a needed item or are having difficulty with another employee for one reason or another.

An esteemed architect, writer and inventor held this epiphany on creating change:

> *"You never change things by fighting the existing reality.*
> *To change something, build a new model*
> *that makes the existing model obsolete."*

Buckminster Fuller

Why aren't systems the first-place leaders go to for change?

I believe the reasons this: Leaders don't take the time to develop the organization's systems:

Sometimes a leader comes up with a great idea, yet it didn't go anywhere because there was little support for what was suggested.

Systems look boring. Creatives sometimes resist systems because they fear it will adversely change the culture. They fear either the new system will eliminate a family feeling or it will eliminate a nurturing culture.

Systems don't need to be created by a leader. Most systems implemented in the organizations I lead came from someone I supervised. Employees are the people most impacted by something not working as well as it should. Ask your employees what they would change or how something could be better. Employees will respond once they know you are listening and open to their opinions and thoughts. Concern some leaders have: How much resistance will this new system get from employees? Will people participate?

Instead of resistance, a well-thought-out system should provide relief. However, if the edict comes from on high to do things a certain way, I can almost guarantee your employees will not totally buy in to the order for change or may even attempt to sabotage it.

This is why almost every new system we come up with resulted from an idea an employee provided and did not come from a supervisor.

The leader's role in implementation of systems

Always remember, action is everything!

If anyone believes leaders simply make pronouncements and everything falls in place, this is clearly a misconception and is not truth. A true leader first formalizes a plan, creates a narrative around the plan and then implements it. However, this is just the beginning phase.

The next stage in implementation is accountability. To implement any plan, participants must understand and agree to the new system. They don't need to like it. However they do need to implement it with integrity.

After implementation, a leader can either conduct a study, wander around, hold informal discussions or look at results data to determine whether the new system is working as conceptualized. My suggestion? Do all four things!

Remember, systems are like habits. Do you know someone who tried to quit smoking? Generally, the individual with this goal in mind must be focused on the end result. They have to do new things and be uncomfortable for a while. They must consciously do new things to prevent the craving for a smoke from taking over. Much is the same with Systems. The old ways will take over if the system is not given a chance to create a new way!

For leaders, the overall goal of systems is to have tasks taken care of with predictability. Your finances, your hiring, marketing, etc., all need to have a system you can count on.

As if seen from a 30,000-foot level, a leader should be able to observe the ebb and flow of an organization. Unless there is some crisis or an emergency loss of an employee, the systems should remain in place while the organization runs smoothly almost all of the time.

There are times, however, when you will lose a key staffer or encounter a major crisis such as an unscheduled audit happens. This often throws an organization into turmoil. A solution to these moments requires having depth as a factor in your organization.

Depth is accomplished by having your key employees backed up by other employees whenever possible. Backups must know at least 80 percent of whatever the missing key employee knows about the job. You will be surprised how well your organization will be served simply by having this one step in place.

The second thing most systems do is help you scale up. If you must be involved with every decision, or your systems are not sound, then you will not be able to scale up or grow your organization. Does this mean that you can't expand? Of course not. However, whenever you do expand or grow, it could end up being a car wreck if your systems are not designed well. To scale up, you must have the capacity to grow larger. If your systems are not in place, you will not know how much work your employees can accomplish.

When you must rely on a key employee the world seemingly revolves around, the organization may not be able to grow as quickly. Especially if this employee resists the vision of leadership. If there is no system in place for this eventuality, then there is a different sort of problem. When you scale up, it is usually because someone requests it or you find an opportunity to make your organization stronger. When you have systems in place, they will give you a competitive advantage. In most cases, you will have relief when your systems are implemented, your people are in agreement and key people are knowledgeable about how things are supposed to work.

A good system will reach a sustained flow in about four to six weeks.

As a leader, you will need to monitor this new way of doing things so it becomes a habit and is ingrained into your organization. Leaders are often overwhelmed by thinking every agency likely needs a dozen or more systems in order to function. Happily, this is a myth!

What you must do is address key issues or problem areas and then design a system to solve each one. Usually, when one system is created, it will solve a multitude of other problems.

One time, our office manager brought me an issue: She and her staff were frustrated because they were not in sync with social workers whenever a child was placed in our agency. She wanted to move forward with an appropriate placement instead of waiting for permission from a social worker.

Her frustration was palatable. This leader knew our foster families better than most of our social workers. It took one meeting for us to create a system where she could contact families on her own instead of waiting for permission. This system helped make many more effective placements at a faster pace this allowing us to take in more children and help them settle into a foster home. We soon gave our office manager specific boundaries on what she could and couldn't do while retaining permission to act when it was appropriate. This one system relieved tension between social workers and administrative staff as well as creating a more healing and supportive transitions for the children being placed.

In the organizations I lead, my goal is to train staff on how to make decisions and provide them with the appropriate criteria for how those decisions should be made. I don't want everything to hinge on me. I have always wanted to provide more services for those in need.

We could not grow as an organization if every decision needed to go through me. My goal is for the organization to be able to function without me and still do things well. In the meantime, I want to be looking at and designing more programs for those we could serve.

My focus is to eventually not be involved in the micromanagement of day-to-day decisions. I advise most leaders to take this advice to heart. However, I do make it very clear to my subordinates exactly what decisions I must be involved in and what things I need to hear about from them.

After years of leading agencies, I soon realized whenever we had problems with our organization's performance, it is because of poorly functioning systems.

Systems do not need to be complicated. Neither do they need to be designed by someone with a Masters in Business Administration. What is needed, however, is the ability of people to recognize and admit there is a problem. Defining the problem is first, followed by gathering feedback, observing, suggesting a solution, obtaining buy-in from others, and implementing a new procedure to produce the desired result.

Contrary to the expectations of many leaders, the primary way leaders can improve an organization is to look for problems! Looking for problems is key to improvement and innovation. When you interview new employees and ask them about the onboarding process, you might get responses similar to these:

"I didn't know who to talk to after I was hired."

"I didn't know which desk was mine."

"I didn't really understand my compensation package."

You obviously don't want this to happen in your agency! However, if you look around, it might already be happening.

The gift here, you can make a better impression on new hires by taking their concerns or complaints and creating standards and systems. This will impress your new hires. My opinion is this: Employee retention starts on the first meeting with whomever is doing the hiring. As a leader, we should always be in pursuit of new innovations and improvements! Just a word of advice here: Do not make the new system complicated!

"Genius is the ability to reduce the complicated to the simple"

C.W. Ceram

One of the simplest ways to improve something is to find out who among your employees or volunteers is performing above expectations. The next step is to study the core things they are doing differently than anyone else. Then create a system for all of your staff to reflect the standards the most productive person is using.

The first steps in developing a system are these:

Define the problem

Determine who the problem affects

Listen to emotions

Ask the employees involved, "What would be the best situation?"

Interview and listen to all involved.

Ask each person for a solution.

Question those involved how changing this situation may be the answer or how it may cause a problem for someone else or another department.

Implement the new system and gather reports over the next 30 days as to how the new system works. Generally, it is good to give permission for those involved to tweak the system if everyone involved agrees and permission is granted by the leader, who is ultimately responsible for the results of a system.

An important part of making a new system work is to hold the leader responsible for keeping the system working. Systems, like habits, take a while to become part of an organization's culture.

There will usually be one person who cares about the new system being implemented because it affects them the most. This person will help hold the efficacy of the new system as well as give you the most accurate appraisal of how the system is or is not working.

How to Overcome Obstacles:

Understand Pareto's Law: Pareto's law says only a small number of the things you do bring you the greatest reward. For example: revenue production. We all need to focus on those key things.

Define the Problem

If you can't define the problem, any attempt to solve a problem will be inadequate and generally must be revisited. It is not unusual for leaders to not look for the problem. I have often told a leader, based on what I am hearing, there is a problem in such and such an area. Those leaders who do not want to find themselves in uncomfortable situations will generally come back to me and report, "There really wasn't a problem."

Leaders need to act as meticulously as surgeons when seeking to find a problem. Don't be afraid to open a patient up, see what can be seen, cleanse the wound area, then assist in healing the situation!

Accept what is, then act.

Determining whether a system works or doesn't requires careful observation, measurement and analysis.

Here are some indicators that a system may be failing:

1. Inconsistent or Poor Outcomes

Failure to Achieve Goals: If the system consistently fails to meet its objectives (e.g., production targets, financial goals, customer satisfaction metrics), it's a strong indicator that something is wrong.

Unpredictable Results: A well-functioning system should produce consistent, reliable results. If outcomes are erratic or vary greatly without clear reasons, the system may be flawed or poorly designed.

2. High Levels of Waste or Inefficiency

Resource Waste: A dysfunctional system often wastes time, money, materials or labor. If you observe excessive waste or inefficiency, the system may not be operating as intended.

Bottlenecks and Delays: Constant delays, bottlenecks, or process slowdowns indicate the system is struggling to function efficiently.

Identifying when a system doesn't work effectively requires careful observation, analysis, and feedback from various stakeholders.

Diagnosing when to create a new system:

1. Consistently Poor Outcomes

Failure to Meet Goals: If the system consistently fails to meet its intended objectives (e.g. productivity targets, quality standards or customer satisfaction metrics), this indicates something in the system process is not functioning as it should.

High Error Rates: Frequent mistakes, defects, or rework indicate inefficiencies or flaws in the system, especially when these issues are pervasive across different areas.

2. Low Morale and Engagement

Employee Frustration: When workers are consistently dissatisfied, stressed or disengaged, it may be a sign the system is overly complex, burdensome or doesn't provide them with the tools and support needed to succeed.

High Turnover: Increased employee turnover often reflects dissatisfaction with the system, especially if employees cite frustration with processes, lack of incentives or unclear expectations as reasons for leaving.

3. Inefficiency and Waste

Bottlenecks: If the system regularly experiences delays, bottlenecks or excessive wait times, it's a sign workflow isn't optimized. Identifying where slowdowns occur can pinpoint areas for improvement.

Wasted Resources: Excessive waste of time, materials or effort is a sign the system isn't operating efficiently. This could be due to poor planning, lack of training or unclear procedures.

4. Lack of Flexibility

Inability to Adapt: A rigid system cannot respond to changes — whether in market conditions, customer needs, or internal challenges — and will likely fail in the long term. Systems need to be adaptable with new information, technology and circumstances.

Resistance to Change: If the system is resistant to improvements or feedback, it may be outdated or too entrenched in a particular way of working which no longer suits the organization's needs.

5. Misaligned Incentives

Counterproductive Behaviors: When employees engage in behavior to undermine overall objectives (e.g., cutting corners, gaming the system or focusing on short-term gains), this often reflects misaligned incentives. The system may reward behaviors not contributing to long-term success or organizational goals.

Inconsistent Rewards: If incentives do not consistently produce the desired outcomes or if they reward wrong behavior, the incentive structure within the system needs to be re-evaluated.

6. Customer Complaints and Feedback

Negative Customer Feedback: Regular customer complaints about service, product quality or responsiveness indicate the system does not meet external expectations.

Loss of Customers or Clients: A decline in customer retention or satisfaction is a clear indicator the system isn't working as expected, especially if the loss is attributed to service or product delivery issues.

7. Lack of Accountability and Ownership

Blame Shifting: If problems are frequent and no one takes ownership of resolving them, it indicates a lack of accountability within the system. A well-functioning system should have clear roles and responsibilities.

No Feedback Loops: A failing system often lacks effective feedback mechanisms. Employees or managers may not receive the information needed to adjust and improve performance.

8. Overcomplexity

Confusing Procedures: If the system has too many steps, redundant processes or is overly bureaucratic, it will slow down operations and frustrate employees. Simplifying the system can lead to better efficiency and morale.

Difficulty Training Newcomers: When onboarding or training new employees takes an unusually long time due to the complexity of the system, this suggests processes are not intuitive or streamlined.

9. Misalignment with Organizational Strategy

Contradicting Organizational Goals: A system working at cross-purposes with the broader organizational strategy (e.g., focusing on short-term gains at the expense of long-term growth) is unsustainable. The system should be reviewed to ensure it supports the overall mission and strategy.

10. Data and Metrics

Lack of Reliable Data: If the system does not produce reliable actionable data, it becomes difficult to measure performance or diagnose issues.

Conflicting Metrics: When key performance indicators (KPIs) or metrics conflict with one another (e.g., one part of the system is optimized for speed while another requires thorough quality checks), this indicates misalignment within the system itself.

SET YOUR STANDARDS HIGH

I undertook a unique approach towards developing my organizations by creating standard operating procedures or Standards.

Therefore, from the very first day, I started asking myself, "What practices or standards should we employ and why?" I decided instead to create a program of services to meet or exceed the highest standards offered by our competition. When it came to standards, I wanted to set the highest bar for our entire region. As I made it past the first six months, we began to gain momentum. We started to land some referrals for fostering children and we were actively recruiting qualified foster parents.

As the years evolved, I continued to bring stability by consistently monitoring how we did things. This kept us moving forward in a predictable way while simultaneously reducing errors. It also meant we were providing a higher level of service for our clients than they were used to receiving from our competitors.

My first action was to eliminate any barriers preventing parents from becoming foster parents. For example, we found out most agencies in our area were charging potential parents a fee to obtain background checks. It costs less than $20 to obtain a live scan or background check, yet other agencies were charging parents up front for a background check. Only if they passed the background check would the agency reimburse parents for this cost.

Our observation: This created a barrier for parents by adding yet another bureaucratic step for them. Instead, we decided to pay for background checks for every parent interviewed when we decided to move forward with them.

Removing barriers is a powerful tool for leaders!

When you remove barriers, your people feel taken care of and the organization generally runs more smoothly.

This is one example of an approach we took. More importantly, however, by doing so we created a new standard. The standard we created was to eliminate processes, functions and any policies creating barriers to obtaining our services. Every organization has certain practices of doing things, yet the reasons why are most often no longer remembered. Typically, those legacy practices are no longer needed and are simply performed out of habit because "We always do it this way."

Below, you'll see some of our systems and standards we created when we transitioned from me doing all the placements to having my staff assist me. Sure, it is Spartan, but we know it works.

Standards for Placing Children:

In the case of our prospective foster parents, we wanted to eliminate every possible barrier requiring a parent to use brain calories before deciding to move forward with the process. Our system standard is to follow up with a foster parent during the first night of any placement. We call to see how things are going for the child and also the parent(s). We believe quality support is necessary. We then inform the county and agency social worker how the first night went and relay any needs identified either by the child or foster parent.

We quickly realized a second barrier was rising among our younger clients who were simply trying to get comfortable in a new home and possibly in a new school.

Many times, children being placed in a foster home don't come with adequate clothing or shoes. Out of the thousands of children placed by the organization where I was CEO, I clearly remember a 5-year-old girl who arrived for placement wearing a pair of oversized adult cowboy boots, a blouse previously belonging to her grandmother and a pair of short pants she had to hold up with one hand so she could cinch up the waistband as she walked. Quite often we receive children dressed in clothing or shoes clearly intended for someone else, possibly even an adult.

Since foster children will most likely be attending a new school after placement, we want to make sure they feel good about what they wear and help minimize the awkwardness of being a newbie on campus. Our system now gives our new foster parents $100 per child to purchase clothing before they start attending a new school or return to their old school. Before we place any child, we assess the child's needs to make sure they have what they need in terms of clothing, hygiene supplies, etc. We also inform the foster parent about the child's situation, any special needs such as allergies or physical limitations and other relevant information. We share all the information we have with the parents. We include the child's medications, food preferences, fears and interests. then, we encourage the foster parent(s) to go shopping and buy each foster child appropriate clothing and shoes similar to what other children in the same community were wearing to school.

This was the right thing to do on several levels. First, the parents received immediate funds to buy the child's clothing. Second, the child was provided with new clothing and shoes in the proper size and style which helped them realize the foster parent cared for them. The child was then able to go to school dressed in new clothes and feel better about themselves.

Systemizing generosity for every placement creates a standard of generosity to help each child feel better about a lousy situation in their personal life. We always strive to place children with a family enabled to do what is right for the child, especially if the foster parents receive two or three children at the same time.

Systems should be developed based on the best practices for any messages you want to convey to clients and the resulting actions you want to implement. A good question to ask yourself: How do I want our organization to be perceived? What standards or values do we desire? How do we create appropriate systems to accomplish these goals?

In the book ***Checklist Manifesto***, author Atwul Gwande talks about how medicine is improved by having standards and then make sure those standards are verified to improve healthcare in impoverished countries. His calling was to make sure the world's medical standards improve and death rates diminish.

Standards can easily be established around work quality. Obviously work standards are one of our most important areas of emphasis.

What does it mean to have a standard? Creating a standard can be as simple as getting people together to ask, "What is our standard for . . .?"

If you are talking about welcoming trainees, you may want to create a standard for how you onboard a new employee. This may cause you to ponder what other standards you desire.

For Example:

How do you want to orientate a new employee?

Who will do the orientation?

Will the employee have a mentor for their first 30 days?

Will you give them swag?

How will you have their work area set up?

What level of service are you committing to giving your employees?

When is an intervention needed for our employees?

Will safety training be involved in the onboarding process?

Onboarding is very important in the process or system to orient new employees to the existing culture or standards expected. When done well, it helps determine the new employee's trust in the organization. This will also translate into how comfortable the new hire or volunteer will be in his or her new job.

Our organization quickly adopted as its Standard to pursue the top tier of quality in our industry and then surpass it. To do this, we needed to see what the best organizations were doing, then match or exceed their actions and standards until we could put those organizations in our rear-view mirror by creating even higher standards.

Another standard in our organization is to consistently take calculated risks to innovate, create or develop iterations or variations to expand services. For our organization, we like to take the high road as a standard. This usually comes about only after we ask ourselves, "What is the right thing to do?" and "What is the best thing to do?"

One standard to aspire for is to never show bias towards anyone. Another standard might be to remain loyal to people even when they are not present. Honesty should be a standard for organizations. We do this by admitting when we are wrong and apologizing quickly and sincerely for the mistake. It is important to have a standard of how you will respond to your clients, even the ones who are the most difficult to please. A value which many organizations with integrity exhibit is to always respect the dignity of others.

What is the difference between a standard and a system?

Standards are the minimal starting point for performance in an area we are addressing.

Systems, on the other hand, are how we will accomplish a task. By establishing what you want something to look like or be like needs to incorporate the how part, which often includes a system to make a standard happen. Some companies may have adopted best practices borrowed from the Society for Human Resource Management (SHRM).

While you were reading the prior questions, I'll bet you came up with some ideas of your own. Perhaps you added some of your own standards. Or possibly, you hadn't given much thought to the issues of onboarding.

Although the subject at hand is onboarding, standards should be created for all areas of your business. In the past, I experienced not having an onboarding system and it is not a pretty sight.

I was directing facilities for developmentally disabled clients in a residential setting. When I was first hired, there was on ongoing crisis within the organization. Several key leaders recently quit and I was hired to replace them. From day one, we were short on employees. When I made time to review the records, I discovered the organization recently experienced a 300 percent turnover of employees in the past year.

After the first week, I was exhausted trying to put out fires. We had two more people quit and many of our personnel were serving clients without the assistance of a necessary co-worker.

I went to senior staff and asked them why we were experiencing such a high turnover rate. The reply from staff was somewhat crusty. After speaking with them, I came up with a theory of why people quit this job and why the turnover was so high. My theory: All new employees should receive extensive training. The second key part of training was to have a training person on shift with the new employee for their first three shifts.

Once we set this as our standard practice, we solved our problem of extreme turnover. For the next year, our turnover rate was below 30 percent. Moving from 300 percent turnover to 30 percent turnover in a year was a massive change. Not only did our clients benefit, our administration and supervisors also benefited. We worked our way out of a crisis by creating a Standard. Setting standards and backing them up with great systems allows you to have more time to tend to other issues.

Leadership does not mean you are getting away from problem solving. However, it does mean you are using problem solving to create additional value for your clients. It is also the means we have of identifying barriers we can eliminate because our authority is to make life better for our employees and clients!

I love creating systems! I know that's a weird statement. However, I know every good system created means I no longer need to be involved in that area of our agency except to address issues when the system is not working or someone is not using the system the way it was designed.

My hope is our employees grasp the value of each system and realize how much effort it saves. Perhaps they will only realize how a system eliminates tension or hostility between colleagues until someone does not follow the system. When enough employees become upset, they will demand the system be followed and remain loyal to what has worked successfully.

Standards and Competition:

Having systems reflecting the standards you want to meet will give your organization a competitive advantage in the workplace. If two agencies are similar and operate more or less the same way, how will one reach a competitive advantage? The answer: By having different standards which are lived out through well designed systems.

INNOVATION, NOT STAGNATION

Innovation must happen in nonprofits desiring to grow, be financially healthy and remain relevant to the changing world around them. Very few organizations will be doing the same things exactly five years from now. If they did, this would be a sure sign of stagnation.

Our industry has gone through amazing changes in the 25 years since I first founded our nonprofit. The services we started with have diminished due to legislation. In fact, if we simply remained in general foster care as an agency, we would have shut our business down several years ago. Instead, we looked ahead and chose to participate in other services similar to those we started with and expanded from there.

Our first expansion was into another region. In the same year, we expanded into providing mental health services. Several years later we expanded again, this time into transitional housing for youth who were just leaving foster care at age 18.

Our innovations in this arena were to find all the realtors in the areas we served, then we began to create our quality standards. Some youths were not ready to live by themselves so we created some assessment tools to see which youths would be okay to live alone and which ones would be served better by having a roommate.

We set goals for youths to be either in school or working and our social workers focused on assisting our youths in moving forward.

An innovation is a new method or way of doing things. We noticed many organizations in our field were lax in working with landlords. At first, when our youth encountered problems, the landlords would evict our clients. We knew most landlords wanted our youths to be successful. Therefore, we needed to establish methods designed to provide us with notice whenever one of our clients was having a problem. We would then set up a meeting between the landlord and our client to remedy the problem.

Our response to problem solving helped our landlords reduce their stress. This allowed us to move new clients into their vacant properties as well as develop more contacts for the future. We knew one bad experience might cause a landlord to take the attitude that this working arrangement was over. Instead, we used the experience of mediation to prove to our landlords we would be supportive of their needs as well as of the needs of our clients.

This strategy worked incredibly well and we soon became the largest provider of these services in an area the size of Washington state.

We also noticed our clients with children sometimes experienced tough times doing regular activities. For example, one of our social workers said the moms were having a hard time getting to the laundromat since many of the apartments did not have safe laundry facilities nearby. Some of our clients previously experienced some traumatic times in their lives and were sensitive to potentially unsafe situations. This left our transitional-aged young mothers with the choice of leaving their babies at home alone, which was unacceptable, or taking the baby with them to a laundry facility.

As a way to keep our young mothers safe and to provide an immediate solution, we purchased portable washers which were easy to hook up in an apartment. This also allowed the parents to keep a steady supply of clean clothes ready for themselves and their young children.

Innovation requires listening intently to what is being told to us. With limited resources, our agency couldn't do everything at once, so it was important to solve the most important problem first. Sometimes this meant we had to come with a method of solving a problem.

It has always been my mission to think through what we are doing, develop the program and then begin to ask ourselves, What can we do to improve the program? It is not a one-time thing. We need to be relentless about improving everything we do.

There is an acronym CNEI which stands for Constant Never-Ending Improvement. I am a big proponent of continual improvement.

When I start talking about competition, many of my colleagues who run similar organizations become uncomfortable. The truth is, if you are continually looking at how you can improve everything you do, your competition will soon be in your rear-view mirror. Our preference is to create, not compete.

The reason other organizations do not continually look at improvement is that it requires work! Directing staff to look at problem issues and areas where the system is bogging down or could be improved requires sensitivity because others may begin to feel leaders are not appreciative of all the hard effort already given. The gist here is creating a culture of appreciating what has been done as part of the goal towards constant improvement.

By constantly improving what you do, your organization will quickly become the first choice of your clients and the community. Your competition will not have a chance if you provide quality services while focusing on removing barriers or solving problems for existing clients. When done consistently, you will truly be in tune with what is going on with your clients and desire to develop seamless services for them.

When we create an environment where the focus of service is on our clients, people who are clients of other agencies want to join our agency. Before we agree, however, we ask these potential clients who are with a different agency to first explore working out their problem issues with their current service provider. We do not recruit from other organizations. However, if our competitors are unwilling to serve their clients to the highest standards, then those clients certainly have a right to meet their needs by migrating to our services.

To implement innovation, my advice to all leaders is to request regular reports from your subordinates to explain how they are innovating and working to improve the quality of their division and the entire organization. Innovation will give you the security you need, the funding you need and the ability to be the leading service provider in your area. Meeting your clients' needs and having them feel valued is the ultimate goal in developing quality services.

"One of the tests of leadership is the ability to recognize a problem before it becomes an emergency."

Arnold Glasow

Innovation:

Now it's time to have fun! It's time to innovate.

I know some of you are going to say, "The best have already innovated. How are we going to build on what they are doing?" The answer is this: You are going to start creating now. You are going to do the things you come up with. Being curious will take you into the land of innovation when you ask yourself: "Why are we doing things this way?" and "Is there a better way to do things?"

You will also find things in need of innovation are the frustrating or redundant tasks which typically come with high cost and offer a low benefit to the organization. Take those things and ask yourself, "What would be a better way to do this?"

For example, I was reading about co-branding and wondered how it might work within our child service agency. The first place I looked was in the areas where we were already fundraising. Every year we donate approximately 150 new bicycles to give to our foster children. Most of these bicycles are generously collected and donated through the efforts of our local Starbucks network of coffee shops and their clients.

The first year of this program, we asked for donations to purchase enough bikes for the children. Since some of the bicycles received were pre-owned. We also asked for cash donations to repair them. However, as I observed the foster parents picking up the bicycles, I realized we were not really meeting the needs of our foster clients. This was confirmed almost immediately when one of our snippety foster parents who had not done any work to help get us bikes said to me, "Why are the kids getting refurbished bikes?" Her complaint was not helpful, yet it was an important point. She did give me something of great value to think about.

So, we innovated.

The next year, I made a commitment to find new bicycles for all of our foster children. Our foster children truly are victims who are precious to me. Throughout their lives, many of these children were lied to, disappointed and received far less love, kindness and material things than most of the children they played with at school.

I remembered seeing advertisements during the Super Bowl and one of those ads was for the Salvation Army. The advertisement which cost several million dollars for a 15- or 30-second spot, was sponsored by Doritos. It hit me. We could do the same thing, yet do it locally.

My recruiter and I discussed the possibility of reaching out to the eight Starbucks stores operating in the three regions where we provide client services. We decided to ask them for donations of new bicycles or money to purchase new bicycles for our foster children.

I still remember our first meeting with five of the Starbucks managers. Starbucks managers believe in supporting the local community. Store managers are encouraged to investigate the local community to see how each outlet can align with existing causes and organizations. Store managers then determine who they want to work with.

Based on research we did and relationships we built, we were able to partner with a total of eight Starbucks outlets the following year. We collected donations at Starbucks and the donations from their customers allowed us to purchase 150 new bicycles for our foster children.

Our youngsters were delighted when we pulled up to their placement homes to deliver these bicycles. Our parents also saw the immense love we have for our foster children. This innovative partnership went a long way towards creating a deep culture of care and support for our families even as the foster families developed greater trust in us.

Our next venture was to bolster the local cancer awareness program. Their leaders asked us to be involved and also asked us for a donation to their cause. We said yes, then asked whether we could partner with them at their annual fundraising and awareness event. We were the first agency of our kind to partner with this nonprofit organization. We love the cause and our involvement lifted up our team members because we could contribute to the community through another nonprofit organization.

We soon discovered the leaders of cancer awareness programs were often young dynamic women from the community. Most of them were cancer survivors or providing care for their family members impacted by cancer. They welcomed us and we arranged to be consistent with their color scheme. We quickly became a valuable part of their outreach program.

When you look around, you will soon notice we all need to be helping each other.

Through these innovations we were able to generate much more community exposure and support. We were featured on the local broadcast news, in newspapers and magazines as well as on social media. This innovation was also about branding and marketing. Branding is all about getting maximum exposure in a positive way so members of the community who never heard of us before become aware the need for more foster parents. These young, committed women saw our need and helped us add to our foster parent base.

Most recently we partnered with a major production company whose mission is to put on a Christmas show for children and families at a local venue. They feature some incredible Christmas lighting and holiday music we knew would appeal to our children and their foster parents. I was also looking for a unique way to bless our employees during the holiday season. Mostly, I wanted to give a great experience to our foster parents and their children while reducing the amount of effort on my staff who were hosting a series of Christmas parties or dinners for all of our clients.

We partnered with this production company and the synergy was incredible. In fact, some couples interested in becoming foster parents came to the event and were impressed by our culture, our parents and how our organization served its people.

In year two, we partnered with one of the premier insurance companies in our region. Their clients were mostly small businesses. We hosted nearly 1,000 business people with a special event. Once they found out about us, those small businesses quickly became generous donors and supporters of our homeless program for high school youth as well as contributing to our bicycle gift drive.

Whenever we find similar events to increase our exposure within the community while also blessing our foster families, the children we serve and our employees, we will do it again.

Before we enter into these joint ventures, our goal is always to get the biggest bang for our investment of time, effort and money. We always ask ourselves these questions first:

How can we get more exposure from social media and news media?

How can we bring in some of our stakeholders as guests. For example, invite the Starbucks teams and their families.

Can we do this event in a better manner?

MANAGEMENT BY WANDERING AROUND

I was in college when I heard about a breakthrough book, **In Search of Excellence: Lessons from America's Best-Run Companies**, by Tom Peters and Robert H. Waterman, Jr. (1982).

I've always been a fan of top leaders doing management by wandering around organizations, whether it be General Colin Powell or Howard Schultz, American businessman and former CEO of Starbucks.

Because I can't paint or play the piano, my favorite art form is understanding organizations and producing results, which in my opinion is as close to art as possible for me.

My finest work involved developing ideas and implementing strategies to serve others better. Only later was I able to turn my creative abilities to turning around struggling organizations. Yes, I know this sounds weird. However, I believe this later work was some of the most important I've accomplished in life.

Devising great management ideas or writing a book to explain the inner workings of how to get maximum results in an organization are as important to me as convincing people to see an exhibit of Tutankhamen's Tomb. Of course, my discovery pales in comparison to the burial arrangements for King Tut. Yet, I am far more excited by insights into changing people's lives or making an organization more effective.

In Search of Excellence was a book which helped me in my first job as Director of a drug and alcohol treatment center at a local hospital. I grabbed onto an idea borrowed from the book which served me for more than 40 years of leadership. The idea was Managing By Walking Around. It was transformative for me because I didn't know what a leader was supposed to do. My immediate supervisor was located in Los Angeles, an eight-hour drive away. The night before, my supervisor left me in charge of a new hospital-based drug and alcohol program after spending only two hours on my training. My supervisor then began talking about this great insight, "Denial is not a river in Egypt." As a recovering person himself, he recounted numerous platitudes about the recovery process. The bulk of this lecture was about as useless as the denial statement.

Then, he left and I was on my own. In fact, I didn't know where my office was on the unit. It turned out to be in the janitor's broom closet. This was a major organization and the drug and alcohol program was literally jammed into a 22 bed wing of a hospital owned by one of the large multinational medical organizations.

Fortunately for me, I did have the first management book I ever purchased as well as a staff comprising a medical director, nurses and counselors to serve our clients. The concept of managing by wandering around was so valuable, I've ended up using it in every leadership position I've held since then.

On the unit, I learned to spend time at the nurses' desk or visiting with the doctor whenever he did rounds. I also spent time in the counselors' offices to see what issues they experienced. I must admit, my presence in a counselors' office made them a bit uncomfortable at first. I'm sure they either thought they were in trouble or curious as to why I was observing them at work.

To make my employees more comfortable, I initially show interest in any pictures of their family members on display around their desks. Then I discuss any hobbies they enjoy or simply ask them how they are coping with the job.

After some small talk, I then ask what is on their mind or what is most challenging for them in their job? Whatever the question, they gradually start to open up and talk about what is really foremost on their mind. For example, if they said, "I'm frustrated with a situation, but it's okay," I would encourage them to elaborate. If they alluded to issues involving another employee or their supervisor, I would simply remain quiet and continue to listen.

I made sure not to jump to any conclusions on how to fix any of these things. Instead, I listened to them and asked questions to probe further.

Many times, these sessions would lead me to insights towards creating a solution or making changes based on the information I received. It might involve implementing a new system or, if I uncovered the ineffectiveness of a leader, I could help coach the leader to be more effective.

One afternoon, the counselor was sitting at her desk as I wandered into her office. She looked a little stressed, so I asked how her work was going. She wanted to run something by me.

"Of course," I responded.

She began by saying she hoped she wasn't being too judgmental or overthinking something.

"What is it?" I asked to encourage her to be more open and trusting.

"Well, some of the older clients are concerned about one of our young volunteers. He is a very attractive young man who volunteers once a week to take our clients to local Narcotics Anonymous meetings," she related.

The counselor was concerned this young volunteer was showing too much interest in a few of our young female clients. His attentions were beginning to be a distraction, at the very least. More importantly, his advances might potentially become a much larger problem if he physically or emotionally hurt any of our clients. Such interactions would seriously reduce the success of these young women in our program, she cautioned.

"I might be wrong here, but this situation doesn't feel right," the counselor added.

"I feel bad about bringing this up!" she ultimately confessed to me.

I assured her I would remain discreet as I continued to evaluate the matter and I would keep her name out of my report, for which she thanked me.

After my investigation, I grew increasingly aware and even more suspicious of our young volunteer's behavior. I eventually discovered some proof of his inappropriate behavior towards some of our young female clients. Very quickly, I was able to make sure he was no longer able to have any contact with our clients. I was able to do this in such a way it didn't expose any private conversations or create more drama.

Management by wandering around often gave me current information which then helped me make decisions and thwart problems. I learned early on, my primary job as a leader was to solve problems. I learned to use management by walking around as a way to solve problems when they were still small instead of waiting for something more dramatic which likely would have consumed many more productive hours.

Management by Wandering Around (MBWA) is a concept developed more than 50 years ago. It is a tool still used effectively by some of the most successful CEOs in the business world.

Howard Schultz, former CEO of Starbucks, regularly made a point of personally visiting 25 Starbucks locations every week.

MBWA helps great leaders know what is going on in their company by going where people work, relax or congregate. Whether it be walking through restaurants or going into offices or factories, these leaders go and speak with workers, not managers and experts. They desire to meet with the people who actually put together the products, cook the food or provide client services.

Why do they do this?

I think they wander around so they can see for themselves the things you can't begin to know simply by sitting behind a desk in an isolated office. The very things data and charts can't tell you. Yet, many of today's leaders fail to use this simple, powerful tool. Leaders who use MBWA, however, find it beneficial. These involved leaders usually find their employees appreciate the boss's attention and the access this provides. Leaders soon discover their visits actually can increase productivity.

I also find it helpful to reinforce our organization's goals and values. I am able to solve problems before they stop our employees from efficiently accomplishing their tasks.

Once, when I was visiting our counseling center, a key staff member appeared to be very tense.

I sat down with her and enquired how things were going. Initially she expressed some frustration. However, when I asked what challenges were preventing her from accomplishing her work load, she told me the most frustrating thing for her and another co-worker was a need for some occasional overtime pay. I asked why she hadn't requested overtime. She indicated she was concerned about costs and believed management would be reluctant to approve any overtime.

Interestingly, I am frugal and try to keep costs down. However, I usually grant employees overtime when it is necessary for them to complete their daily tasks.

These employees likely forgot the permission previously given and were left swimming in frustration. I asked how many extra hours she needed in the next 30 days to fix the situation. She indicted "about 15 hours should do it." I immediately approved this amount of overtime.

This kind of interaction is a common experience when I do my MBWA. I am very intentional and try to gather as much information as possible. I have found innovations I would never have discovered if I waited for people to come to my office.

I have made improvements in the visitation of children, making the workplace much more pleasing for our employees as well as finding out new opportunities that I would have missed. Leaders can solve a lot of problems by discovering them while wandering around. Yet, most of a leader's time is spent in a private office. To combat this, I generally walk into another person's office and, if appropriate, sit down in an empty chair and strike up a conversation.

Some of the most amazing things I've observed is how much extra work some employees are doing on behalf of our youth. One of our social workers takes our teens to a ceramic shop where everyone paints a vase or a plate and enjoys a dessert while waiting for the glazed pottery to emerge from the kiln. I didn't have any idea this was happening. However, when I learned about it, I realized the social worker wanted more than anything to make a difference in the lives of our youth.

I once went to our office and was offered toast by several 7- and 8-year-old girls who were working with a loving older staff member. This staffer took it upon herself to start a girls corner when young children from several foster homes come to the office for counseling. The girls learn to socialize and serve each other simple things such as a piece of toasted bread.

Girls who have been in multiple placements in their lives are now learning how to be calm and socialize in a way no one ever expected.

I wander around every day when confined to office work. I don't ask a lot of questions unless an issue is presented to me. However, I can immediately see who is stressed, who is not doing well and who is making great inroads in serving our clients. Many times, I will also find out about the children of my staffers or realize their spouse is working on a job site out of town or hear about a personal loss the staff member is experiencing. When I truly listen to someone and show I care, many times this simple act allows them to turn the corner on a tough time they are going through.

It's not because of anything I do. Mostly, I want my staff members to know their leader cares for them and I grant them permission to discuss personal situations with me. One side benefit, I have never been asked for more time off work or a request to extend a critical deadline when I manage in this manner.

Instead of an employee having to request these things, I have preemptively granted an employee time off or reset a deadline once I hear what my people are going through.

Always respectful of honoring my time, one of my managers asked if she could speak with me about one of her co-leaders. We enjoyed a great conversation for more than an hour about her future plans including her desire to return to school. We discussed work issues as well as what she and her family were doing for Christmas.

As our conversation neared an end, I asked, "Is there anything else?"

As I expected, she indicated a significant issue with another employee whom she was concerned about. I listened to her, asked a few questions and learned more about the situation.

Eventually, she told me about a situation I most likely would not have learned about until it became a much larger problem. When things become larger problems, I'm usually left with only one choice. I much prefer having the opportunity to handle something before it grows into a wildfire.

I really didn't enjoy hearing about the issue, but part of my job as CEO is to handle problems and confront uncomfortable topics. In these instances, I usually handle my stress by eating dark chocolate.

This one instance of learning something when managing by walking around (MBWA) reinforces why this one act is so essential. Wandering around is my most effective way of finding out valuable information. Furthermore, when people trust you, they will tell you what you need to know even though it is not always what you want to hear!

Waterman and Peters discovered similar practices used by successful CEOs and other leaders who all spent time in the field with employees. Many of them, including Starbucks CEO Howard Schultz, often go behind the sales counter to engage in discussions about new innovations. They also hear from employees whether the great ideas coming down from the pipeline from higher ups are really working or causing more problems than resolving issues.

Waterman and Peters also found out the CEOs and leaders who wandered around were able to solve problems with more ease. They were also able to inform other leaders why some ideas or practices work well and others don't.

This makes sense to me because when I seek out another person's perspectives, especially from employees, I begin to appreciate and see the world through their eyes! This type of management always suited me because I could go talk with an employee, go back to my office, and create objectives I want to accomplish.

Another way to manage by walking around is to hold an unstructured conversation with a specific individual — more as a coaching session — and ask several questions to see where the conversation goes. As you do this, you will find employees feeling more at ease with you. As a result, they often will show you things they are working on and what they are accomplishing. They will often tell others about this interaction and others will soon find it easier to approach you as well.

When I speak with other leaders about this concept, sometimes they are cynical. When they reply, "I try to do that, but I just get busy," I usually remind them of Starbucks CEO Howard Schultz and others who use this technique and how effective it has been for them. Schultz supervised more than 20,000 stores, yet made a point each week to visit at least 25 stores in whatever location he found himself. Imagine the perspectives he could share back at headquarters when he met with other Starbucks executives and board members. Who would you rather trust in deciding corporate direction, solving problems and creating innovations? It wouldn't be the person who never goes out to see what is really happening! I'd rather it be a person who hears directly from people who deal with customers to create the company's desired goals.

Innovations come about more often than not by people who are the end users of a product, process or providing a service. In my experience, the people who I supervise will usually not be ecstatic when describing something which works for them. Usually, they will act more subdued and say "it works good." More than a few will likely look at you blankly until you remind them of the way it used to be. It's just as well. I would rather see things work and the end users think it was their idea or innovation. In the end, they are probably justified in this way of thinking. I simply was fortunate to be in a position to make sure their ideas were implemented.

One interesting thing to be aware of is employees may think their concerns are too insignificant to discuss with the CEO. When something is mentioned to me, I take this as a clue of its importance to the employee. This is when I begin to unpack the problem they are casually bringing to my attention.

Usually, I discover the problem they think is insignificant actually has the potential of disrupting our entire operation or ends up costing us time and money to fix. In some extreme cases, allowing the situation to continue may even cause some of our employees to leave.

One skill leaders need in their tool box is the ability to listen. Your subordinates will always listen to you because you are the boss. However, when bosses do all the talking, it is difficult to learn anything new. Learn to keep your mouth shut while others speak and encourage them to explain things you don't fully understand. This will soon build a bond between you and your employees. I find it helpful to listen at least 70 percent of the time whenever I am managing by wandering around!

Many times, this technique allows me to share with employees some strategy I've already discussed with our executive team which will soon bring about the desired results employees seek. Obviously, this shared information must be appropriate and timely.

When someone gives me a great idea or I implement one of their innovations, I do my best to give them appropriate credit. This lets them know their ideas and efforts are significant and management has the integrity to give employees deserved recognition.

Deposits and Withdrawals

Managing by walking around builds stronger relationships by using deposits and withdrawals.

Steven Covey, author of ***The 7 Habits of Highly Successful People,*** mentions this tool which can completely transform an organization. Based on the idea of bank transactions, leaders who take from employees will soon find out there is nothing left in the account of goodwill. However, if they are generous with praise and recognize effort, the goodwill account will remain healthy and able to withstand most any difficulty.

The great thing about solving problems or creating innovations based on feedback from employees who are blessed for their contributions is the further removal of barriers which prevent them from completing their job tasks more easily and with less stress.

Whenever leaders are able to solve a problem — be it a personnel or process issue — they are preventing a worst-case scenario from developing. This is important because the worst-case scenario will almost always cost an organization undue time and stress which sometimes results in one or more of employees choosing the exit door rather than deal with the turmoil.

Relationships are similar to bank accounts even though our deposits and withdrawals do not involve currency. In any relationship, spending time by listening, caring and showing compassion are most valuable. A deposit of this type leaves the other person feeling better about you than they did before.

A withdrawal occurs when an interaction leaves the other person feeling something was taken away from the relationship. Withdrawals include distancing yourself from others, not being around when needed, showing a lack of attention or making demands without any deposits being made.

This generally ends up in a situation where there is strife, conflict or someone loses.

Sometimes, I prefer to interact with others in a coffeehouse or restaurant when someone needs my full attention. Remaining in my office can prove distracting and I want to fully listen to my employee's concerns.

100 PERCENT RESPONSIBILITY

Leadership requires leading a life which reflects your perception of taking 100 percent responsibility for your organization and people.

My mentor Henry and I usually talk twice a month. On one occasion, Henry asked me, "How are things going for you, Mike?"

"Well, I feel like I am pushing a string across a table," I replied.

"What are you dealing with?" he asked.

This prompted me to recount a difficult personnel issue I was trying to solve.

Henry then asked me his famous responsibility question.

"Mike, how much of this problem are you responsible for?"

Without a doubt, I was in for another of Henry's leadership lessons.

"Well, probably 30 percent," I replied.

"Wow! That's too bad!" he responded.

I recognized from his subtle yet placating tone this was leading up to Henry's favorite speech. It is how we coach our foster parents to respond to a child who misbehaves or breaks a rule.

"What do you mean, Henry?" I responded a bit too impatiently.

What he said next changed my paradigm on responsibility forever!

"If you were 100 percent responsible, you could probably solve the problem," Henry countered.

His response stung. However, I wanted to know what was behind Henry's response.

I asked him to explain how one of my employees and her supervisor being unable to resolve an issue was my responsibility. Henry explained, even though the employee and supervisor were not under my direct supervision, I still could bring about a solution. As we talked through this problem, I realized most problems with employees are because we either hired the wrong person, did not train the person thoroughly enough or they did not receive adequate coaching, supervision and accountability.

While I realized I probably shouldn't interfere with one my leaders supervising an employee, I actually could take action to help remedy the situation. My part in the equation was to coach the supervisor in areas where she was deficient. I realized, too, in the future, we needed to do better at on-boarding employees while also creating a better system of accountability.

My job as a leader is to solve problems. Fortunately, I don't always have to be the only one to solve the problem! As a leader, I can make things happen and should be able to get things done through other people.

"Highly proactive people don't blame circumstances,
conditions or conditioning for their behavior.
Their behavior is their own conscious choice."

Stephen Covey

The concept of "100 percent responsibility" can transform how leaders can take action and achieve heightened effectiveness, even when initially it appears circumstances seem outside their purview. This philosophy centers on internal agency, we can move beyond blame to proactive, solution-oriented action.

By adopting 100 percent responsibility, you acknowledge that everything in your life and circumstances is, in some way, is you're doing. This perspective removes all excuses and eliminates external blame, placing you firmly in control of your life.

Being a leader is a process and a mindset. It's not something given to you. Leaders must step into the role and claim it. In many situations, there are bound to be grey areas. In leadership, when we are supervising other leaders or even clerical staff, there is often a grey area of responsibility.

For example: My clerical staff received an irate call from a donor or a client we serve! The call was unusual in its scope and emotional quality.

The question I needed to ask of myself: Do I respond or should I allow the clerk to handle the situation?

The important factor to me is knowing when to respond as a leader and when do I allow others to respond to situations. I believe it all depends on how your organization is set up and how well you have prepared your people to respond.

What we need to avoid is having people we supervise handle problems which are clearly ours to decide. Otherwise, your team members will eventually wonder why you are absent on handling problems. You definitely do not want them wondering whether you lack courage or you are sending them into situations where they are out of their league or acting above their pay grade.

Here are five things you can do to become the highly effective leader you desire to be:

Ruthlessly eliminate blame and excuses by focusing solely on your response. The core of 100 percent responsibility is the unwavering commitment to not point fingers or make excuses, even when it seems justified.

> *"As long as you think the problem is out there,*
> *that very thought is the problem."*

Stephen Covey

1. Own everything in your sphere of influence.

Take absolute ownership not just for the tasks you are directly assigned, but for everything that impacts your mission or your team's success. This means internalizing that if something goes wrong, it is ultimately your responsibility to find a solution or prevent it, even if others are involved.

2. Focus relentlessly on solutions, not problems.

When faced with a challenge, shift your energy from dwelling on "Why did this happen?" or "Whose fault is this?" to "What can I do about this situation right now?"

This proactive approach transforms you from passive to solution oriented.

3. Cultivate a proactive and growth-oriented mindset.

An ownership mentality means being proactive and solution-oriented, foreseeing issues and preparing solutions rather than merely reacting to problems. This survivor mentality views challenges not as insurmountable obstacles but as opportunities for growth by believing in one's ability to overcome adversity. As a leader, foster an environment which emphasizes learning from mistakes as well as continuous improvement.

4. View challenges as opportunities for growth rather than obstacles or inconveniences.

Emphasize the importance of learning from mistakes and continuously improving. Equipping everyone in an organization to engage in an ownership mentality without fearing failure will take any team from where they are towards where they want to be.

I must admit, there were times when I didn't take responsibility and doing so did hurt our organization.

In my early years of leadership, I kept waiting for someone else to rescue me or do the things I didn't like to do yet were necessary for the success of my organization. One of those things was my lack of doing deep work in reviewing regulations, contracts, potential opportunities and items requiring me to slog through the details. Eventually, I learned most of the information necessary. However, I did not push myself to know as much as other leaders knew.

I would be in a meeting and try to wing my way through by following the thoughts of the loudest person in the room. At the very least, I made it through those meetings and was able to come up with some good decisions. More than once, however, I missed an issue or a detail in a contract which cost us dearly in the future. Yet, most of the time I got away with it because I was the leader. Even then, I knew when I failed myself as well as my entire team. This cost me my integrity.

Eventually, I came to the place where I realized the more research and planning I did at the beginning would end up being beneficial in the long term because I laid a solid foundation from which to base my work decisions. As my style of leadership changed, I also began to realize so did my goals. I no longer wanted to just get by. Instead, I desired to know everything the new situation required. Gone were the days of being cognitively lazy, I was driven to live in the land of integrity.

If you are training your employees to take on more responsibility, whether to determine if they have the grit to negotiate or the ability to deliver even in a tough situation, there is one thing to be understood by all involved. Coaching at this level can be powerful. However, there must be integrity in the situation. Leaders need to take responsibility, give guidance and provide oversight for issues involving their staff under the following conditions.

- Whenever staff is not prepared to handle the situation.
- Whenever a lower-level leader wants to avoid the issue.
- Whenever the matter will clearly be damaging for a lower-level leader's integrity if they do not want to confront the issue.

Identifying Strong Leadership Traits

Great leaders use all or most of the items tabulated below. Look them over and see which traits you could incorporate into your own leadership style.

Always have a plan:

Be responsible for your relationships. Be responsible for your company's results. Don't blame!

Learn how to use the power of narratives! Grow accustomed to feeling uncomfortable!

The Basics of Leadership:

Every leader needs to find out what three to five things they must pay attention to every day. These should include the things a leader needs to do in order for the agency to move forward. However, a leader also should include the things employees need to accomplish to fulfill the agency's goals.

One of the things I focus on every day is to identify any barriers my staff members encounter which only upper management can do something about. I also focus on customer service issues including who is not being served to our standards. Next, I pay attention to numbers. Not just financials, but the number of clients we are serving as well. This also should include keeping track of donations, donors and any fund-raising efforts.

Another paramount concern for me is the health of my staff. This includes both emotional and physical well-being. Next, I pay attention to what else is happening today which might affect the organization's future. I never worry about having the right answers all of the time. I realize how much more valuable it is to ask the most penetrating questions. It's very hard to lead when your main desire is to always be right. When you insist on being right all the time, you're eventually going to find out you're wrong on some things, especially if you hang onto the notion of always being right. In the end, you'll end up with a crisis.

Stop trying to have all the right answers

In the long term, it is often more productive to come up with great questions.

Pay attention to how your identity shapes your actions.

Who you think you are often shapes your actions. Influence is a leader's responsibility and a tool which should be used often. At a deep level, study influence.

Listening to and understanding others is a large part of building influence.

THE RELUCTANT LEADER

One of the things I've noticed in the nonprofit world is the absence of leaders!

Janice was a person whom I selected to lead our agency into a new area of service. Her promotion was decided not because she was an extraordinary leader. Rather, it was because she held the right degrees, loved the clients and wanted to see the lives of our young clients changed. It didn't hurt matters when I noticed Janice was likable and others thought highly of her. She often obtained amazing results even when her clients were very resistant. She never gave up on anyone.

Wrongly, I sometimes assume all people want to make the most of their career and move up the leadership ladder. When I first approached Janice, I inquired whether she was interested in leading our new program focused on finding housing and case management for transitional age youth. These are the youths who have a long history of foster care and are about to age out of the system once they turn 18 and are no longer considered a minor.

Funds were available to place these youths into their own home, provide case management services and also provide guidance with the goal of helping them become responsible adults. We would continue to support them as a way to help break the cycle of poverty, abuse and failure in which many of our clients are trapped.

When I spoke with Janice, it became clear she was adamantly not interested in taking on the leadership role for this new venture. However, I knew Janice possessed a unique sense of humor because we worked together for more than a decade. I reminded her I needed her to lead the program and offered to be there to see her through any difficulties.

She eventually agreed. However, she always reminded me she wasn't the real leader of the program. It took more than two years before she owned the concept she was the program's leader.

Now, after almost a decade of providing leadership for this service, she has become one of the outstanding leaders in our industry. She successfully placed our first two clients who were very rough and exhibited little capacity to live on their own. In new programs such as this one, it is not unusual for the counties we work with to place their most challenging youth into such programs. I hope it is because we have proven time and again exactly what we are capable of and also because we do a good job.

Janice did help these two young men. Her success further affirmed our agency's abilities with the counties in which we operate. We are now the leading program of such services in northern California. Meanwhile, Janice continues to innovate, market and solve problems as well as any MBA from Harvard or Stanford. I sometimes chuckle when I hear her using phrases I used with her when observing her strategic thinking on how to provide the best possible service.

To me, this is ample proof these methodologies do bring out the best in people. Especially for people who never thought of themselves as leaders yet eventually realize they can be leaders and excel while doing it! They simply need some guidance and support whenever the leadership mantle becomes too heavy to bear by themselves.

THE PROBLEM OF MISALIGNMENT

When organizations are aligned, they usually develop a strategy to coordinate efforts, resources, procedures and systems towards a common goal. Ideally there should be both horizontal and vertical alignment where departments, teams and individuals work together to achieve primary objectives. If alignment is lacking, your organization may suffer from poor employee relationships, miscommunications, a lack of accountability and an unwillingness to take on more responsibility within the organization. This point of view will eventually affect deployment, strategy, execution, employee coordination and synergy.

How misalignment starts in an organization:

Alignment usually gets out of whack whenever leaders fail to honor their people by recognizing their value publicly or by failing to give their employees clarity on the organization's vision.

A lack of organizational alignment often stems from one or more of several fundamental issues. One common problem is when leaders are operating under a false illusion everything is going smoothly. Leaders consistently overestimate strategic alignment whenever they mistake message delivery for message absorption, agreement and commitment.

Just because a leader makes a great presentation doesn't mean everyone else buys in to the message. Sometimes, leaders must determine how much of what they say at meetings is truly being understood by those on the receiving end of the communication.

Leaders may also mistake silence from employees for agreement and commitment, especially when team members are afraid to speak their minds due to a lack of psychological safety. This creates a culture where the CEO makes it clear by their actions they expect only supportive messages in favor of the CEO's strategy. Therefore, valuable messages which could prevent future problems are seldom heard by the CEO or anyone else in executive management.

When a leader communicates a strategic imperative or gives direction, he or she should check whether the message was absorbed by a majority of the people in attendance at a meeting or on the receiving end of an electronic message.

When a message is poorly communicated, it can more easily cause confusion and resistance. Rumors can start and misinformation may follow. True leadership which changes lives will require a leader to find out how his or her team has accepted the communication. This is much more than giving tacit approval or people responding affirmatively simply because they want the leader to approve of them. One simple answer to this problem is for a leader to ask people what they learned from the communication. Only the best leaders will humble themselves in order to hear responses different than what they believe was said.

If the leader sends out an unclear message, it may result in a lack of buy-in on the part of most employees. Research clearly shows as many as 95 percent of an organization's employees don't understand their company's overall strategy. When this happens, there is an interpretive gap. This gap in understanding allows employees to interpret for themselves how any message applies to their own work, which can quickly lead to myriad different versions of a single strategy on the part of different people within the organization.

When there are deficiencies and misalignment occurs, leaders may stop believing in the new vision or strategic direction. Research shows 75 percent of managers do not believe they have any personal stake in the company's strategy. This is often due to a lack of sufficient development and training, not incompetence.

At times, leaders who rely on information such as data reports, KPIs or budgets will simply assume behavioral alignment will logically follow, which is not always the case. There's also a tendency to prioritize strategic speed over strategic depth by rushing out policies or mandates to be met in a short time frame without any time for reflection, discussion, questioning or contextualization at all levels.

Leaders often use misguided measurements such as activity, project completion or meeting attendance without assessing whether actual strategic understanding or buy-in occurs. This creates a false sense of alignment.

Leaders also should thoroughly understand how remote and hybrid work models can significantly challenge an organization's alignment. External factors including geopolitical conflicts and economic uncertainty, combined with internal issues such as burnout, can also contribute to disengagement and, consequently, cause misalignment.

How Misalignment Affects Employees

Lack of alignment profoundly impacts employees regardless of their leadership aspirations. This is usually evident when decreased engagement affects productivity. Misalignment directly impacts employee engagement, making them less inspired to give their best effort at work.

According to one study, only 26 percent of employees feel engaged at work and only 22 percent plan to remain in their present role. Lack of meaningful recognition and clarity around expectations are usually the most significant drivers of these attitudes. This leads to low morale, frustration and disengagement.

Poor relationships and communication misalignment will eventually lead to poor employee relationships, miscommunications and a lack of accountability. Within teams, this can manifest as back-channeling, gossip, workplace politics or silo-based thinking.

When there is a lack of clarity and motivation, employees receive inconsistent instructions based on different interpretations of strategy, conflicting priorities and performance metrics justifying rewards to individual or silo performance rather than broader organizational results. This lack of clarity around what's expected can lead to a workforce which only shows up because they must, rather than being motivated to drive the organization forward.

Resentment and powerlessness often happen when employees believe leaders are simply dictating orders to them. Resentment quickly leads to a reduction of commitment to goals. This often happens in an environment where decisions are imposed without employee input.

What Misalignment Does to an Organization

The consequences of misalignment extend throughout the entire organization and will eventually affect its performance and viability. Strategy Execution Failure occurs when a company's vision has almost no chance of success because leaders at every level aren't fully aligned. This, in turn, makes hitting targets difficult and can actually derail strategy execution, team engagement and organizational performance.

Without buy-in from leaders as well as employees, even a brilliant vision and strategy makes no difference.

Misalignment affects resource deployment, strategy execution and employee coordination. This can slow operations, increase inflexibility and create sluggish programs which result in project delays, budget overruns and further communication breakdowns.

Inconsistent execution of a vision can soon erode a brand's trust with consumers while leading to negative bottom-line impacts. For example, inconsistent pandemic-related safety measures eventually caused serious issues in many organizations large and small.

Misalignment can also create stagnated growth and contribute to a lack of innovation. An organization with alignment issues is usually unable to implement necessary changes and risks falling behind better aligned organizations. A culture where resistance to change is the norm will soon discourage new ideas and creative thinking.

Each poorly managed change initiative decreases the organization's overall capacity for future changes, thus creating a downward spiral of increased resistance.

Organizations usually must pay a premium price when they are misaligned because they often have difficulty executing new strategies efficiently and effectively.

Symptoms of an Organization Not Aligned

Several symptoms indicate a lack of organizational alignment. The following is a list of symptoms you can easily identify whenever there is misalignment in an organization.

- Poor employee relationships and miscommunications.
- Inconsistent instructions based on different interpretations of strategy.
- Decision protocols are not clear, and decision making is slow.
- Discussions and decisions happen outside of meetings, not in them.
- Meetings often circle around rote status updates and regurgitated decision-making.
- Meeting topics are predictable and repetitive.
- Accountability and performance problems.
- Conflicting priorities across silos and departments.
- Stated priorities aren't adequately funded or resourced.

- Performance metrics and expectations reward silo performance and individual achievement ahead of organization-wide results.
- Leaders focus on short-term results which lack a long-term view.
- Decreased productivity or performance.
- Low employee engagement.
- Increased complaints or negativity.
- Higher absenteeism.
- Nostalgia for the old ways.
- Minimal participation in change initiatives.
- Compliance without commitment.
- Formation of resistance coalitions.
- Power struggles create confusion around roles and responsibilities.
- Back-channeling, gossip, workplace politics, and silo-based thinking due to a general lack of psychological safety.

How to Fix an Organization's Alignment

An executive director must adopt a comprehensive and empathetic approach to fix misalignment. Usually, this is done by recognizing alignment requires intentional and ongoing effort. The process to fix organizational alignment usually involves strategic planning, effective communication, employee involvement and strong leadership.

Strategic Planning for Alignment:

Assess Change Readiness: Before initiating any change, analyze past successes and failures, identify potential resistance hotspots, gauge leadership alignment and commitment and determine resource availability.

Get a Top-Level, Strategic Understanding of Goals: The executive team must agree on the company's main goals, strategies, and interdependencies based on core values and competencies. Objectives and Key Results (OKRs) can be used to create actionable, ambitious and data-driven goals.

Create a Compelling Vision

1. Develop a Comprehensive Communication Strategy
2. Communicate early and often what's changing, the context, address concerns, and provide regular connection.
3. Use multiple channels including team meetings, one-on-ones and large group discussions. When communicating, explain the "why"

behind the change and how it aligns with goals. Outline benefits for both employees and the company. Be transparent about challenges to build credibility. Create feedback loops for questions and concerns. Tailor messages for different departments/roles.

4. Involve Employees in the Change Process. It is necessary to pass information down the organization. Communicate the importance of alignment, and outline expectations around collaboration, roles, and goal ownership. Use OKRs to collaboratively create lower-level team and individual OKRs that support the overarching company OKR. Establish feedback mechanisms (surveys, focus groups, suggestion systems). Empower managers as change leaders with information and resources. Involve employees early and often in strategy design and execution to foster ownership and ensure they understand goals, success metrics, and their part in the plan.

5. Provide comprehensive support. Deliver targeted training for new skills. Allocate sufficient resources (time, tools, budget). Dissent is important in an organization. Encourage dissent by creating psychological safety for constructive disagreement.

Constant and never ending improvement needs to be nurtured in an organization.

As you can see, the cost of an organization not properly aligned can be astronomical. If your organization is experiencing misalignment, know you're not the only organization experiencing this. You can prevent misalignment, however, it must be caught early or your organization will suffer the financial and psychological consequences.

ALWAYS MOVE YOUR AGENCY FORWARD

Leaders must make sure to take care of the present even while always taking actions to move the organization forward. It is always easy to get caught up in chaos, craziness and emergencies. Whenever I find myself in this situation, I sometimes fall into the trap of thinking I have too much going on to move my agency forward. However, if leaders want to be successful, they must take action towards what they desire to see and do in the future. In many cases, once leaders have saturated the areas in which they serve, often they decide to diversify.

Have a sense of urgency

Be consistent in your focus of moving your organization to its next level. Make decisions based on what you are able to see in the present as well as what may happen in the future. You must be comfortable about moving on with what you already have going for you.

> *"Be comfortable with moving without all the answers.*
> *Be flexible."*

John Maxwell

You can tell what you want to see in the future by the actions you take today. The evidence of where you want to take your organization in the future is obvious by the actions you are taking today. The risk involves misjudging the cost of failing as an organization.

> *"Tolerating failed experiments is a very specific part*
> *of the excellent organizations who are strong*
> *— and that lesson comes directly from the top.*
> *Champions must make lots of efforts and consequently suffer*
> *some failures or the organization won't learn."*

Thomas J. Peters
and **Robert H. Waterman Jr.,**
In Search of Excellence

To grow, you will sometimes need to experiment with a new way of doing things. To not experiment is to live in fear of what might happen. See what will work or not work for you. This doesn't mean you should put all your reserve cash on red as if you were standing around a roulette table. Take small chances on new ideas. Many times you can spend very little and learn a lot more about what would happen than if you debated whether you should invest larger amounts of money on an idea. Also remember, with possibility, there also comes problems.

REQUIREMENTS OF GREAT LEADERSHIP

Alright, let's take a deep dive into the essence of great leadership and how it's cultivated. As we've already discussed in previous chapters, leadership isn't a static title. It's more of a dynamic process of growth.

Using influence

A great leader can often enter into situations and by using their influence, create an impact for good. To truly understand how great leaders operate, we need to delve beyond mere definitions and explore the active strategies and profound perspectives which drive success. Great leaders don't simply stumble into their roles. Instead, they are intentional architects of leadership development, both for themselves and their team members.

Leaders develop strategies by first understanding leadership is a skill set to be nurtured and enhanced. What you will see in all great leaders is constant strategizing. They are usually thinking about the potential of what ifs. These leaders also can read the clues of the current situation and decide what the best course might be to take in the future.

This involves a systematic approach to identifying those current and future leaders already positioned within an organization. Don't look only at who holds a managerial title. Instead, actively seek out high-potential employees who demonstrate desirable leadership traits. Once identified, these individuals should undergo a thorough assessment of individual strengths and weaknesses in order to identify those areas in need of improvement.

Your assessment shouldn't be punitive. Rather, it should be a solid foundation for tailoring developmental programs designed to cultivate each person's unique capabilities. Great leaders use all or some of these tools and structures to raise up leaders for future growth and development.

The following programs are multifaceted and incorporate a variety of initiatives.

1. Mentorship programs pair emerging leaders with experienced professionals who can offer personalized guidance and knowledge transfer. This isn't just about passing down information; it's about

building a supportive relationship where the mentee can gain valuable insights and networking opportunities.

2. Allowing 360-degree feedback provides a holistic view of a leader's impact by gathering input from peers, subordinates and supervisors. This comprehensive feedback is crucial for creating targeted development plans as it highlights blind spots and reinforces strengths from multiple perspectives.

3. Leadership workshops focus on key leadership competencies such as communication, decision-making and emotional intelligence. These aren't passive lectures. They are interactive sessions to provide practical tools and strategies for real-world application, thus allowing leaders to learn from trainers and each other.

4. Cross-functional projects challenge high-potential employees to lead teams across different departments. This fosters collaboration and adaptability, exposing them to diverse perspectives and enhancing their versatility by understanding the interconnectedness of the organization.

5. Emerging leader programming is specifically designed to nurture individuals showing strong leadership potential. This programming uses coaching to help them build on their strengths and create a road map for ongoing development, effectively creating a pipeline of future influential leaders.

6. Executive coaching offers personalized support for senior leaders by providing guidance and accountability to overcome challenges and maximize potential. This is a one-on-one process tailored to individual needs by helping leaders refine their prioritization, communication, team engagement and change management skills.

7. Action learning projects are experiential and tackle real business challenges thus allowing leaders to apply theoretical knowledge in a practical setting. These team-based projects encourage experimentation and learning from both successes and failures while providing invaluable experience in problem-solving and collaboration.

8. Leadership retreats offer a dedicated space for leaders to self-reflect, build stronger relationships and engage in strategic planning. The combination of formal sessions and informal

interactions fosters a shared vision and a more cohesive leadership culture.

9. Job rotations provide leaders with a deeper understanding of different parts of the business by moving them across departments. This helps them adapt their leadership styles to the unique needs of various teams and individuals.

10. Assessment tools such as Clifton Strengths™ and MBTI® help leaders gain crucial self-awareness by identifying their strongest professional traits and personality preferences. When coupled with coaching, these assessments provide personalized guidance for leveraging strengths and addressing development areas.

11. Community engagement initiatives cultivate essential qualities such as empathy, social responsibility and servant leadership by involving leaders in external projects.

    These experiences can also strengthen relationships within the organization and enhance a leader's influence.

The skills great leaders possess are not innate talents. Rather, they are honed abilities. They exhibit enhanced leadership skills in communication, decision-making and strategic thinking. These skills are continuously refined through development strategies. A leader's ability to influence others stems from a genuine effort to build trust, understand what motivates other team members and create an environment where everyone feels heard and valued. This isn't about manipulation. It's about fostering a shared sense of purpose and direction.

Integrity and accountability are non-negotiable for great leaders. Leaders should act ethically, take responsibility for their actions and ensure their subordinate teams operate with the same principles. In today's dynamic business landscape, the ability to act decisively is crucial. Great leaders aren't paralyzed by uncertainty. They make timely decisions based on available information and are willing to adjust course when necessary.

Finally, resilience defines great leaders in the face of setbacks. They don't view failure as an endpoint. Rather, it is a learning opportunity. Leaders maintain optimism and chart a new path forward while showing support for their team through even the most challenging times.

A NONPROFIT LEADER'S EDGE

The characteristics of great leaders paint a picture of individuals who are both strong and human. In my opinion, leaders also should embrace a growth mindset by constantly seeking opportunities to learn and improve while recognizing stagnation soon leads to decline. Authenticity is their bedrock; they lead with honesty and humility while being true to their values and personality rather than trying to fit into a preconceived mold. Great leaders empower their teams by putting the needs and development of others first while genuinely encouraging subordinates to reach full potential. Humility allows leaders to recognize their personal limitations and actively seek out individuals with greater expertise while fostering a collaborative and effective team environment. They practice transparency by openly sharing information about the organization's goals and challenges even as they foster trust and a sense of shared purpose among employees. Great leaders actively encourage risk-taking and innovation by creating a safe space for experimentation and create an environment where failures are seen as valuable lessons on the path to achieving ambitious goals. Empathy is a cornerstone of a leader's interactions. They understand and share their own feelings and encourage this of their team members. This helps build stronger connections and fosters a more supportive environment.

Leaders should be perceived as fair, reliable and credible. They must earn trust and respect from those they lead. Adaptability allows a leader to navigate change effectively by adjusting their approach and mindset to achieve desired outcomes even as situations evolve. All leaders should demonstrate high moral standards and set an ethical tone for the entire organization. Combining social awareness and a tender heart enables leaders to build strong teams while genuinely caring about the well-being of their members.

The perspectives of great leaders are often rooted in a deep understanding of their role beyond simply directing tasks. Many see their primary function as being of service to their people by adopting a democratic approach to prioritize the needs and enhance support of their teams. Leaders should focus on molding consensus around a shared vision and core values. This will unite their teams under a common purpose rather than solely dictating individual beliefs. The philosophy of leading from behind, empowering others to take the lead while taking responsibility during challenging times, is a perspective embraced by many powerful leaders.

Leaders should strive to create an environment where each team takes ownership of their successes as well as failures. Great leaders prioritize the team's vision and actively involve other team members in the planning process. This fosters a sense of collective ownership and buy-in. Leaders instinctively understand the crucial balance between leading and following. They know when to step forward and when to empower the team to excel independently.

One fundamental perspective a leader needs is to focus attention and effort on the end result rather than simply a series of tasks. By inspiring others to come up with creative solutions, a leader allows his or her teams some autonomy in how a desired outcome is achieved. Continuous self-improvement and a hunger for feedback are integral to a leader's perspective along with recognizing personal growth is essential for effective leadership. The perspective of servant leadership by prioritizing the needs and growth of subordinates ahead of their own is a powerful driver for many great leaders.

Developing high-performing teams is a deliberate process for great leaders.

They go beyond simply assigning tasks and focus on cultivating the potential within each individual.

Their methods include:

- Careful appraisal to understand individual capabilities by providing appropriate levels of responsibility and authority while setting individuals up for success rather than overwhelming them.
- Modeling the way by demonstrating a desired attitude, work ethic and standards will set a clear example for their team members to follow.
- Believing in their team's success and explicitly communicating this belief while fostering confidence and encouraging individuals to rise to or above clearly stated expectations.
- Providing honest and empathetic feedback by acting as mentors and coaches to guide their team members through mistakes while fostering continuous improvement.

- Sharing power by empowering team members to make decisions, solve problems and meet challenges independently by fostering a sense of ownership and accountability.
- Offering public praise to acknowledge and celebrate successes by reinforcing positive behaviors and building confidence within the team.
- Granting autonomy by providing the team with members who have the necessary skills then trusting individuals to execute and succeed on their own fosters independence and growth.
- Focusing on the result, not just the task, allows team members to innovate and find their own path to achieve the desired outcome.
- Understanding the difference between leading and following involves knowing when to guide and when to step back and allow a team to operate independently.
- Serving from the bottom prioritizes the needs of team members while creating an environment where they feel supported and valued.
- Allowing creativity and innovation by fostering a culture where new ideas are welcomed and experimentation is encouraged.
- Developing personal skills first by recognizing self-growth and self-awareness are fundamental to effectively developing others.
- Embracing transformational leadership by focusing on team-building, motivation and collaboration in order to drive positive change and elevate the team's performance.

The essentials of great leadership as enumerated above are the core principles underpinning all of a leader's actions and perspectives. These include setting clear, achievable goals and objectives which provide a road map for the team to follow. It's really all about the ability to make tough choices during difficult times by demonstrating resilience while guiding the team through periods of uncertainty. Facilitating clear and consistent communication is paramount to ensuring everyone understands the vision, individual roles and group expectations.

Great leadership inherently involves the ability to influence others by building strong relationships based on trust and mutual respect. Transparency, when balanced with the need for confidentiality, fosters an open and honest environment. Cultivating a culture by encouraging risk-taking and innovation is essential for long-term success and future adaptability. Demonstrating unwavering integrity and accountability sets an ethical standard for the entire organization. The capacity to act decisively and adapt swiftly to changing circumstances is crucial in today's increasingly volatile business world. Resilience — the ability to bounce back from setbacks and maintain a positive outlook — is a hallmark of effective leaders. Ultimately, great leadership is about creating an environment in which others can excel by shifting the focus from individual achievements to the collective success of the team.

Here are three key takeaways to internalize:

1. **Leadership Development is a Continuous and Multifaceted Investment:** Great leaders understand building leadership capacity is not a one-time event but an ongoing commitment requiring a variety of strategies from formal programs to personalized coaching and real-world experiences. They don't just focus on senior leaders; they actively identify and nurture potential at all levels by ensuring a robust pipeline for the future.

2. **Authenticity and Empathy are Foundational to Influence:** True leadership influence isn't about wielding authority; it's about building trust and connection. Great leaders prioritize authenticity, leading with their values and being genuine in their interactions. Coupled with empathy, this allows them to understand and respond to the needs of their team members by fostering a supportive and motivating environment where individuals feel valued and understood.

3. **Great Leaders Serve to Empower and Elevate Their Teams:** The focus of a great leader shifts from personal achievement to the success and growth of their team members. They actively empower their teams by sharing power, providing autonomy, offering constructive feedback and celebrating successes. Their ultimate goal is to create an environment where individuals reach full potential and drive the organization forward.

In every organization and division there should be a strategy and a vision of what the future should look like.

Strategy versus tactics

Remember, added information will change how you see and do things. Be flexible. However, do not use information to get out of doing something uncomfortable which must be done. Your goal as a leader is to reach clarity about your situation. Leaders need to define reality. Clarity is one of a leader's greatest responsibilities.

Make the complex simple! Try to break down everything to its most simple components. Be intentional. Ignoring intentionality produces poor results!

STRAIGHT TALK

Talking straight and to the point is the most effective ways to create dynamic teams, provide clarity and move your organization forward to accomplish set goals.

Being direct and unafraid lets people know how you think about a situation and sends a powerful message. There are times when speaking from your feelings is the best way of communication. When you do this, be aware of what you say, why you choose to speak emotionally and why you are communicating in this manner.

Most of the excuses for not being willing to engage in straight talk or being fully transparent are:

1. Fear of Anxiety or Negative Morale. Leaders may believe they are protecting their team from stress and worry. The leader may worry about providing information before a plan is finalized may cause dissension. Conversely, the leader may think he will no longer be trusted if he cannot be totally transparent.

2. Such leaders may hesitate until they have more complete content, which in some instances could lead to confusion, misunderstanding or a further lack of trust.

3. Some leaders are concerned about legal, contractual and confidentiality restraints.

   I once terminated an employee who later began to say things which were factually untrue about the incident. When I was questioned about the termination at a subsequent leadership meeting, I declined to respond because it was a personnel issue. As leaders, we need to protect ourselves, our company and anyone close to situations because some situations may turn into litigation.

4. Leaders may want to avoid offending clients or key stakeholders. In my career, stakeholders occasionally make terrible mistakes based on decisions which hurt children. Even though my employees didn't hold the power to make those decisions, they were emotionally stressed and disliked the stakeholders' decisions as well. When I was questioned about the stakeholder's

decision by employees. my response would typically be, "I don't like what the other organization has done, however we lack the power to overturn their decision. In the future I will be talking with the organization and express what we believe would be a better decision. I will make it known how their decision affected us." When dealing with a county agency, I spoke directly with county leadership. If it was a state regulation, I let our state association know and requested they work to change the regulations or policies mandated by the state.

5. Leaders sometimes say things to gain popularity, yet never back it up with any serious intention of action. Leaders may not speak truthfully about a difficulty the organization may be facing in the future. Instead, they give employees a pep talk to minimize the total effect of how a future situation might affect them.

6. Leaders can feel vulnerable and often fail to admit making mistakes. As a leader, I rehired an employee who previously worked for me. I knew I was taking a risk, and in fact, I did some research and found out disgruntled employees who quit and then are subsequently rehired are 60 percent more inclined to quit again. I told my board this may be the case and I shared with key leaders the possibility this might happen. When the employee eventually quit, she said some cruel and untrue things and blamed many people in the organization for her second departure. Once again, I met with my leadership team and took total responsibility by saying, "I did what I thought was right and I take responsibility for the stress this person's actions caused some of my staff."
    Interestingly, my staff felt bad about what I was going through and expressed their compassion and support for me.

Information Overload and Misinterpretation

Some leaders believe sharing too much information is counterproductive. They may worry employees will become overwhelmed, confused or misinterpret the data without any proper context. They also might fear employees will jump to the wrong conclusions (e.g., "We're going bankrupt!") without a full understanding of the business landscape.

I believe leaders should always be able to create a context for transpires. This can happen without talking about the details of an event by focusing on the context.

Lack of Leadership Training and Skills

Many leaders, particularly new managers, may not have the training or skills to conduct difficult conversations with their team members. They may lack the confidence to address tough topics with empathy and honesty, thus leading them instead to avoid those conversations altogether.

THIRTEEN POWERFUL IDEAS FOR TALKING STRAIGHT AS A LEADER

1. **Be clear about intentions and expectations:**

   When communicating, ensure your purpose and desired outcomes are explicit to create a conversation history. Whether in conversation, sending an email or calling a meeting, be clear about what you need to accomplish and what you expect from others.

   Example: "Today, I want to finalize our key objectives for the 3rd Quarter marketing campaign and assign initial responsibilities. By the end of this meeting, I expect each team member to volunteer for at least one key task related to their area of expertise."

2. **Use simple and direct language:**

   Avoid jargon and communicate in a way everyone can easily understand. Great leaders are recognized for their ability to communicate directly and deliver messages with no room for confusion.

   Example: Instead of saying: "We need to optimize our resource allocation to enhance synergistic outcomes."

   Say, "We need to use our money and people more effectively to get better results."

3. **Provide regular and candid feedback:**

   Offer honest and timely feedback, both positive and constructive, to help others grow and gain a shared perspective.

   Example: "John, I need to discuss our 2nd Quarter report which was due last Friday. We still haven't received your report. This delay impacts the entire team's ability to move forward. What challenges are you encountering? What is your plan to get the report completed?"

4. Confront tough issues directly:

Address difficult conversations and problems proactively rather than avoiding them.

Example: "I've noticed some friction in your interactions recently. It seems to be affecting the team's dynamics. I want to address this openly now to ensure a productive working environment. Can you each share what's happening from your own perspective?"

5. Confront reality:

Address the tough stuff directly. Acknowledge the unsaid. Lead courageously in conversation.

6. Clarify expectations explicitly:

Ensure roles, responsibilities and desired outcomes are clearly communicated to avoid misunderstandings. Disclose and reveal expectations. Discuss them. Validate them. Renegotiate them, if needed, and when possible.

Example: "Sarah, I'm assigning you to lead the Alpha Project. The key objectives are X, Y, and Z, with a final delivery date of [xxxx]. I expect regular weekly updates on your progress and the budget allocated is [$xxxx]. What questions do you have about these expectations?"

7. Be transparent with information:

Share relevant information openly and honestly to build trust and keep everyone informed. Be considerate. Ask yourself, "Who else may need to know the information I possess?" Create transparency by telling the truth in a way people can verify it. Get real and be genuine. Be open and authentic. Err on the side of disclosure. Don't have any hidden agendas and don't hide information.

Example: "I want to be upfront with you all. We are exploring some potential restructuring options at the leadership level to improve efficiency. Final decisions are not yet set, however, I wanted to directly share this information as soon as it was appropriate. We will keep you informed as matters progress."

8. **Be courageous and vulnerable**

   Showing you care is important. However, as a leader, be willing to challenge the individual who is tentative or unable to follow instructions.

9. **Authenticity and transparency matter**

   Lead with who you are.

   > **Example:** "We are in a tough situation and I don't have all the answers. However, I am in this with you. I value your point of view and ideas, so let's move forward together to find a remedy."

10. **Practice to care personally and challenge directly:**

    As described in **Radical Candor**, a book by Kim Scott, show you care about individuals while also being direct in your feedback and challenges.

    > **Example:** "David, I can see you put a lot of work into this presentation. Your passion for the topic is evident. However, the data in slides three and five wasn't clearly linked to your main argument. This was a bit confusing for me. Let's work together to strengthen those connections next time."

11. **Be authentic and genuine:**

    Lead with your true self, being honest about your strengths, weaknesses, and beliefs. Start with self-awareness. Leaders become more authentic when they begin by knowing who they are and what they're good at, how emotionally intelligent they are, and how others perceive them. Get real and be genuine. Be open and authentic.

    > **Example**: "We are in a tough situation, and I am concerned. I am dealing with my own emotions about this situation. I know we all have feelings about what is happening, however, we need to express our feelings, define the problem and move forward as a team."

12. **Listen actively and ask clarifying questions:**

    Pay close attention to what others are saying and ask questions to ensure full understanding. Watch the other person. Do not let your eyes wander. Be attentive. Immerse yourself in the conversation. Use clarifying questions to confirm understanding.

> **Example:** "Could you please share with me why you have changed the report format to the board of directors. I would like to understand your perspective."

13. Follow through on commitments:

One of the most important things you can do to engender trust is to follow through on commitments: Do what you say you will do and communicate proactively if you cannot meet a commitment. Keep your agreements. Your employees will allow you to save face when you don't. However, they will not trust you if you continue to break agreements.

> **Example:** I promised my grandson I would take him to his favorite restaurant the next time we went skiing even though I didn't think they offered a healthy menu. The day of our ski trip finally arrived. While loading up the car after a day of skiing, I asked JJ if we could pass on the restaurant stop for this trip. He glumly agreed. However, as we entered the town, I again remembered my commitment. "JJ, I'm going to keep my word because it's what I promised. It is important I keep my agreements or renegotiate them," I said.

WAYS TO ENCOURAGE STRAIGHT TALK
WITHIN YOUR ORGANIZATION

Create Psychological Safety:

Foster an environment where people feel comfortable speaking up, sharing ideas and even making mistakes without fear of punishment or humiliation. A leader should respond supportively even to a dissenting opinion.

> **Example:** "Thank you for sharing an alternative perspective, Mark. It's important we consider different viewpoints as we make decisions."

If everyone is invited to talk and share their opinions, a leader must protect the integrity of this process. When a leader allows someone to be shut down or worse, the leader shuts down the speaker, it may take some time to rebuild trust.

"Psychological safety is a shared belief held by members of a team that the team is safe for interpersonal risk-taking."

Amy Edmondson

Lead by Example

Model straight talk in your own communication. Be direct, honest and transparent.Openly admit a mistake.

> **Example:** "I reviewed the data and it seems I made an error in my initial assessment. I apologize for any confusion this may have caused. Here's how it will be corrected."

Actively solicit feedback and clarification:

Regularly ask for input, concerns and questions from your team. Leadership is not just about what you achieve. It's also what you enable others to achieve. A leader explicitly invites dialogue following a presentation.

> **Example:** "Before we move on, I want to hear your thoughts and any concerns you may have about this plan. Please don't hesitate to ask any questions, even if they seem obvious."

When we paraphrase another person's statements, such as: "Did you mean to say we are making an error in this situation?" we are letting the other person know what we heard. When we ask clarifying questions, we give the other person an opportunity to set things straight and rephrase what they are trying to say.

Reward and Recognize Straight Talk:

Acknowledge and appreciate individuals who communicate directly and honestly, especially when it involves bringing up difficult issues.

> **Example:** Publicly recognize an employee for raising potential risks: "I want to commend Sarah for bringing up the potential risks associated with this new strategy during our planning session. Her directness allowed us to address those concerns proactively, which will ultimately benefit all of us."

Demonstrate Respect:

Genuinely care for others by showing you care. Respect the dignity of every person and every role. Recognizing straight talk demonstrates respect for the contributions of others.

Establish Processes for Open Communication:

Implement formal and informal mechanisms for employees to share their thoughts and concerns, such as regular meetings, feedback sessions, or anonymous channels.

> **Example:** Implement "Ask Me Anything" sessions or use anonymous feedback platforms. Effective feedback mechanisms are crucial for organizational learning and growth.
>
> I once gave out boxes of gourmet cookies to every person who asked me a challenging question

Train and Develop Communication Skills:

Provide opportunities for employees to learn and practice effective communication techniques, including how to have crucial conversations and provide constructive feedback.

Be Prepared to Hear the Truth:

Cultivate a mindset of openness to feedback, even when it is critical or uncomfortable.

> **Example:** A leader responds constructively to uncomfortable feedback. "Thank you for sharing this with me. I appreciate your honesty and understand this was difficult to say. I will need some time to reflect on this, however, I promise to take your feedback seriously."

Listen First, Speak After:

Listen before you speak. Understand, then diagnose. Listen with your ears, your eyes and your heart. Being prepared to hear the truth requires listening first.

THREE KEY TAKEAWAYS FOR TALKING STRAIGHT AS A LEADER

Clarity and directness are paramount:

Effective leadership hinges on the ability to communicate intentions, expectations and feedback clearly and directly. Avoiding ambiguity reduces confusion and fosters alignment within the team.

Trust and psychological safety are foundational:

Create an environment where individuals feel safe to speak honestly, offer dissenting opinions and provide feedback without fear of negative repercussions. This encourages straight talk and builds trust.

Talking straight drives positive outcomes:

While it can sometimes be uncomfortable, honest and direct communication ultimately leads to better problem-solving, stronger relationships, increased accountability and overall progress for individuals and the organization.

LIVING IN THE LAND OF UNCOMFORTABLE

As we have just explored straight talk and summoning the courage to be authentic and courageous, this chapter is about expectations of the leadership position we hold. A profound truth is genuine leadership isn't about comfort; it's about purposeful unease which drives progress. Let's dive into how leaders can cultivate this crucial skill, drawing directly from the wellspring of these insightful sources.

Embracing Discomfort: A catalyst for growth

The very act of leading often requires venturing into uncomfortable territory. Think about it: declaring new futures, reallocating resources, and holding people accountable — these are inherently situations which may generate unease, both for the leader and his or her team. Discomfort can be an asset. It can motivate the leader to be innovative and results oriented. When someone is uncomfortable and doesn't react in anger or hostility, they can use discomfort by purposefully engaging in situations to stretch and transport them into a better place than they've previously occupied.

Honestly, it takes a completely different mindset to be a successful leader. We are required to act courageously when we don't want to and look at things from a different perspective.

Active Engagement:

When leaders embrace discomfort by consciously choosing to step into challenging situations rather than avoiding them, they are creating resilience. When I must do something I don't want to do, I try to change my mind set to one where I will be stronger when I follow through. Realizing I overcame this situation before, when I encounter it the next time, I intuitively know I experienced this before and know I will be successful. Consciously thinking this will help alleviate much of the stress and discomfort.

Leaders Reframe Challenges:

A growth mindset helps leaders see challenges not as threats but as opportunities for growth and improvement. This reframes discomfort from a negative experience to a potential catalyst for positive change.

Embracing discomfort and making it a growth experience is just like any skill, embracing discomfort can be honed through practice. Starting with smaller, less critical uncomfortable conversations can build confidence for larger, more significant ones. Rehearsing difficult conversations can also dissipate fear.

Watch the stories you create about uncomfortable situations. In fact you're better off acting before fear takes hold. You do have a choice: Either allow the anxiety of an unaddressed situation turn into the misery of not dealing with situations when required to act or take action once you formulate a plan.

A significant portion of discomfort arises from the stories we create about what might happen. Leaders can counteract this by addressing difficult situations promptly, before imagination amplifies your unease of the unease of your employees. The sooner you act, the less discomfort you will experience.

Carol Dweck popularized the concept of a growth mindset. Her concept is fundamental for leaders navigating the complexities of today's world. It involves believing abilities and intelligence can be developed through dedication, learning and persistence, rather than falsely relying on those qualities existing only as fixed traits.

Leaders see challenges as opportunities:

Leaders with a growth mindset don't shy away from tough situations. Rather, they view them as opportunities to learn and improve. Setbacks are seen as a natural part of the learning process, not as indicators of inherent limitations.

Making up your mind to aggressively deal with problems and take action as soon as you can to resolve an issue will propel you towards continuous learning and development. You can train yourself to actively seek information about industry trends and best practices, thus enabling you to make informed decisions and adapt effective strategies. This also will develop a culture of continuous learning within your organization and community.

Being creative and innovative will give you confidence to develop new skills and insights. The more you develop unconventional solutions and take calculated risks, the sooner you create a culture of innovation within you and your team. Mistakes should be viewed as learning opportunities.

Embrace Feedback:

Leaders with a growth mindset see feedback as a valuable tool for development, not as a personal criticism. They are open to learning from experiences, even setbacks, while refining their approaches over time.

Model Growth:

Leaders must demonstrate adaptability and share their own experiences of learning and evolving. Recognizing and celebrating effort and improvement, not just achievements, reinforces the value placed on the learning journey.

Establish Norms for Handling Failure:

Leaders should recognize mistakes as growth opportunities and openly share their learned lessons. Failure is not failure if you learn from it.

Failure should be seen as one way of learning. Everything should be seen as a growth opportunity to be appreciated and lived with peacefully

Create Space for New Ideas:

Challenges should be presented within a supportive context, encouraging even wild ideas. Asking tough questions is acceptable. However, always do so with a supportive approach to accept new ideas coming either from you or your people. You do not have to accept and implement every idea, however, there should be a process of birthing new perspectives and ways of doing things.

FOUR TAKEAWAYS FOR EMBRACING
UNCOMFORTABLE LEADERSHIP

Embrace Discomfort as a Path to Progress.

True leadership isn't about avoiding unease. More often, it is about recognizing meaningful growth, innovation and positive change often lie just beyond our comfort zone. Cultivate a mindset to see discomfort not as a threat, but as a signal that you're stretching, learning and leading effectively. Embracing the difficult will make you stronger and less intimidated about what you may encounter in the future.

Build Psychological Safety Through Vulnerability.

Be open when communicating. Create an environment where your team feels safe to take risks, voice concerns and learn from mistakes. This requires leaders to be vulnerable themselves by openly managing their own insecurities and prioritizing clear, empathetic communication. A psychologically safe space is fertile ground for growth and innovation.

Commit to Lifelong Learning and Adaptability.

The leadership landscape is constantly evolving. Embrace a growth mindset by prioritizing continuous learning, actively seeking feedback and viewing every challenge as an opportunity to refine your skills and strategies.

Your ability to adapt and learn in the face of discomfort will be your greatest asset in leading yourself and others towards a better future.

Embrace Discomfort with Intention.

Foster a culture of psychological safety and commit to continuous growth. As a leader, unlock your full potential and inspire your team to do the same. Remember, the most impactful leaders are often those who are willing to step into the arena of unease, not to create chaos, but to forge a path towards progress.

URGENCY IN LEADERSHIP

To become the leader you're destined to be, you must understand the potent force of urgency. It's not about frantic activity. Rather, it is a focused decisive energy to propel you and your organization forward. Let's dissect what it truly means to lead with urgency and how you can harness its power by drawing from these insights.

The Essential Qualities of a Leader Who Acts with Urgency:

A leader who acts with genuine urgency embodies several key qualities:

Vision: They possess a clear and compelling vision of the future and understand the imperative of moving towards it swiftly. This vision provides the why behind the urgency.

Decisiveness: Urgent leaders are effective in decision-making. They weigh information, consider options, and choose a course of action with conviction, understanding that delays can hinder progress.

Communication: Leaders should excel at clear communication, effectively conveying the importance of timely action and aligning their teams around the most urgent goals. This includes explaining the reason why now falls behind the need for speed.

Accountability: They hold themselves and their teams accountable for meeting deadlines and driving results. This creates a culture where timely execution is valued.

Motivation: They are skilled at motivating and inspiring their teams to act with purpose and speed. This involves setting clear goals and providing positive reinforcement.

Courage: Acting with urgency often requires courage to take calculated risks and push beyond comfortable timelines.

Problem-solving: They are adept at problem-solving, quickly identifying obstacles and implementing effective strategies to keep progress on track.

Learning agility: They exhibit learning agility, quickly learning from experiences and adapting strategies when necessary to maintain momentum.

Passion: Their passion for their work and vision is contagious, inspiring others to embrace the urgency.

Embracing Responsibility: Urgency arises when a leader embraces their responsibility to lead and sees challenges as opportunities for growth. It's crucial to differentiate between true urgency and a false sense of urgency which can lead to stress and burnout without actual progress. True urgency is rooted in the importance of the task in relation to the vision, not arbitrary deadlines. If an organization remains in a constant state of emergency, then nothing is seen as an emergency and everything becomes normal.

Eisenhower's Principle for Prioritizing Tasks:

Former U.S. President Dwight D. Eisenhower, articulated a principle for managing workload based on urgency and importance:

Urgent and Important: These tasks should be done immediately.	**Important, Yet Not Urgent:** Tasks set aside to make time for most important goals.
Urgent, Yet Not Important: Tasks which could be delegated to someone else.	**Neither Urgent Nor Important:** Remove most of these unnecessary distractions.

The Eisenhower Box helps leaders visualize their workload and consciously prioritize activities which contribute to their long-term vision ahead of those which merely demand immediate attention yet don't align with core objectives.

Why Urgency is Crucial for Organizational Change

"Urgency is important because meaningful organizational change cannot occur without the cooperation of the affected stakeholders."

John Paul Kotter

Creating urgency is the first step in John P. Kotter's **Eight Step Model for Leading Change.**

John Paul Kotter is the Konosuke Matsushita Professor of Leadership, Emeritus, at the Harvard Business School. He is a published author and founder of Kotter International, a management consulting firm based in Seattle, Wash., and Boston, Mass.

His thesis on urgency is crucial because meaningful organizational change cannot occur without the cooperation of those involved. Leaders must alert the organization to the fact change is necessary and prepare them for the change process.

Here's why urgency is paramount:

Captures Attention: Leaders take actions to capture the attention of critical organizational stakeholders.

Explains Importance: Leaders explain the importance of making speedy changes to the existing condition.

Gains Cooperation: It's the first step to gain the cooperation of management and employees.

Sells the Future Value: Leaders create urgency by selling the value of a future state to stakeholders.

Highlights the Danger of the Status Quo: They make the status quo a dangerous place for stakeholders to remain, often through frank discussions about market realities, financial data and opportunities versus crises.

Honest Communication is Key: A manufactured sense of urgency will be seen for what it is and will doom a change effort. Communication must be clear and honest.

Without a sense of urgency, the organization may become complacent and resistant to the necessary shifts. Leaders must create a compelling narrative that demonstrates why change is no longer optional.

Perspectives on Using Urgency in Leadership

"Without urgency, nothing will change."

John F. Kennedy,
former U.S. President

Positive Driver of Momentum: A healthy sense of urgency, arising from a leader's embrace of responsibility and vision fuels momentum leading to achieved goals and high morale. When an organization achieves momentum. hardly anything can stop it.

Guard Against False Urgency: Many individuals in corporate settings experience a false sense of urgency where managers create artificial deadlines for non-critical tasks. This can be driven by a need to appear busy, exert control or maximize output at the expense of employee well-being. When everything is labeled as high priority, it often means nothing truly is.

Urgency versus Panic: Effective leaders instill urgency without creating a sense of panic. Panic paralyzes while inspired challenge motivates. Leaders can foster urgency by focusing on areas of influence, transparency, hope, engagement and empowerment.

Strategic Urgency: Urgency should be aligned with strategic goals. Leaders need to balance immediate demands with long-term vision, thus avoiding the trap of constantly reacting instead of planning. Systems and routines can help manage this balance.

Situational Urgency: The perception of urgency can be subjective and context dependent. What feels urgent in a life-or-death situation differs drastically from corporate tasks like spreadsheets. Imposing a sense of emergency on non-emergency situations can be detrimental to morale.

THREE TAKEAWAYS ABOUT URGENCY

1. Urgency in leadership is driven by a clear vision and the critical need to move forward. It demands decisive action, effective communication and accountability well beyond simply setting arbitrary deadlines. Leaders must discern between what is truly important and requires swift action versus what is merely presented as being urgent.

2. Eisenhower's Principles provide a powerful framework for prioritizing tasks. By emphasizing the allocation of resources towards important, non-urgent activities which contribute most significantly to long-term success, it becomes easier to strategically delegate or eliminate less impactful tasks. This prevents leaders from being perpetually consumed by the urgent at the expense of the truly important.

3. Creating a genuine sense of urgency is the foundational step for leading successful organizational change by highlighting the

necessity and benefits of the change while underscoring the risks of inaction. This requires honest and transparent communication to gain stakeholder buy-in, contrasting with the detrimental effects of manufactured or false urgency.

OWNERS VERSUS HIRELINGS

As a CEO, I often think about who else in my organization might be a good leader. This act of reflection usually takes me back to my childhood days of living on a ranch in Colorado.

One night a barn caught fire just before 11 p.m. The barn held a lot of stored hay as well as three horses. I was around age 6 and was roughly awakened by my older cousin, Emory, 14, who began yelling throughout the house, "The barn is on fire."

It was a cold night and Emory noticed the fire when he rousted out of bed to get a drink of water and saw flames flickering outside the front room window.

Emory and Uncle Franklin ran towards the barn and Emory continued inside even though the barn was now engulfed in flames. He knew the horses must be freed from their stalls or they would burn up. Uncle Franklin began to collect hoses with which to fight the flames. Emory disappeared for what seemed like 20 minutes and we all grew more and more concerned for his survival. Suddenly, we saw one horse bolt through the open barn door with portions of its mane on fire. Seconds later, Emory emerged leading two other horses to safety.

My sister, brother and I hung back with my aunt to watch as my cousin quickly traversed the 100 yards from the barn to the house because of the fire's intense heat.

I tell you this story because Uncle Franklin and cousin Emory demonstrated the difference between an owner and a hireling. My uncle didn't own the ranch. He was the farm's manager. However, Uncle Franklin and cousin Emory each acted as owners by risking their own lives to save the ranch's three horses. Their commitment to something higher than themselves is forever imprinted on my memory and it is they whom I wish to emulate.

We find similar situations in business. Usually, employees don't involve themselves with life and death decisions. However, people in business are often asked to give their attention, resources or kindness on behalf of the operation.

We realize this most readily when we desperately need something from a supplier, agency or even our work colleagues. Especially when our urgent request for assistance is met by apathy or indifference. We certainly prefer the times when our pleas for help are greeted with empathy and we are guided to the very product or service we need. This second type of person desires to meet our expressed needs and will often do whatever it takes to fulfill our request.

Therefore, when I am looking for a potential leader, I look at whether they react as either an owner or a hireling when it comes to the business or organization. When I choose employees for potential leaders, I want them to consider themselves as owners as well as willing employees. They should learn to care as much as I do about the organization and its clients. It should be evident to employees and leaders alike, the needs of our clients and the organization are equally important.

From a faith perspective, Jesus said it best:

> *11 "I am the good shepherd.*
> *The good shepherd gives His life for the sheep."*

John 10:11 (NKJV)

> *12 "But a hireling, he who is not the shepherd,*
> *one who does not own the sheep,*
> *sees the wolf coming and leaves the sheep and flees;*
> *and the wolf catches the sheep and scatters them.*
> *13 The hireling flees because he is a hireling*
> *and does not care about the sheep."*

John 10:12-13 (NKJV)

In fact, the ones who take ownership care about what they do as if it were their agency or their family and do everything they can to serve in such a manner they sometimes get asked, "Are you the supervisor or director?"

People with this mindset will serve you well!

On the other hand, sometimes we inherit or hire people who act like hirelings. They limit themselves when helping others or those they supervise. They are generally selfish. At times you might hear them say, "That's not my job" or "I don't get paid enough to do that."

The hireling is only concerned about their own comfort or what others can do for them. They may also use others to further their own selfish ends. You will also not see them as eager to jump into solving problems. Usually, they are more concerned about how to avoid the situation and will sometimes blame others for the negative consequences of their inaction.

It is also good for leaders to ask, "Am I behaving like an owner or a hireling?"

The owner cares about employees, the business, other stakeholders and are all-in on helping make the business a success.

The hireling thinks differently and with a different mindset. They generally lead only out of ego or selfishness rather than in a manner beneficial for others, the organization as well as the mission.

Every organization has its share of owners and hirelings. Therefore, leaders should look closely before promoting someone to leadership and consider whether you believe the candidate is an owner or a hireling. In my experience, there are shepherd leaders and hireling leaders in every organization.

Which one are you?

DON'T LEAD FROM COMPASSION!

I can well imagine anyone seeing the title of this chapter might wonder whether this is the right book for them. However, let me reassure you by providing a living example of why leading from compassion is not always the best way to lead.

When I first began my agency which takes care of foster children, one event nearly stopped me in my tracks. One of my social workers notified me of a biological parent who discovered where his child was placed in foster care and went to visit the residence. Before I could reach the location, the biological father fled after making threats against the family and stating he would be back to unlawfully take back his child.

When I arrived at the scene, my social worker was still consoling the foster parents who were mortified this biological parent was brazen enough to come to their home and threaten them and the child.

As I listened, I quickly learned the police were not notified and none of our safety protocols for foster children were being followed. In this situation, the social worker is supposed to immediately contact the county's Social Services personnel, then notify the police and finally, find a safe place for the child or children to stay. It was now a half-hour after the confrontation and the only thing our social worker accomplished was to console the family.

Believe me, I realize consoling foster families is a high priority! However, in our protocols, the safety of all concerned is a higher value. All of our social workers are trained in these protocols.

What if the biological parent reappeared with a weapon or with a group of other people to take physical custody of his child. If the police are not contacted, the foster family is vulnerable to injury or worse.

Immediately, I instructed the social worker to follow our protocols. She was resistant because the parents were shaken. I advised her the protocols would likely take five minutes to follow, however, this task was the highest priority. Once the county Social Services agency and the police were properly notified, she would then be available to console the parents, but only after we created a safety net around the family and the child in placement.

Leadership is not unlike an emergency response team coming upon a traffic accident. While there is noise, excited people and business going on around them, their duty in a crisis is to assess the situation, bring stability, support those in need and create an area of safety. If the EMT's start instead by consoling victims, the victim's family members or talking to bystanders, their first response attention is going to be lacking and people could end up being more severely hurt or damaged.

It is a leader's job to lead, not to console or express compassion when leadership is needed.

Wise Compassion Leadership Matrix:

Quadrant 1: Low Wisdom, Low Compassion Ineffective Indifference. Leaders often are disengaged, make poor decisions and lack interest in expressing a concern for others.	**Quadrant 2:** Low Wisdom, High Compassion Compassionate but Ineffective. Leaders exhibit empathy and care for others yet lack strategic insight and decision-making ability.
Quadrant 3: High Wisdom, Low Compassion Wise but no compassion. Leaders have skills, knowledge, make effective decisions, yet lack empathy and concern for the team's well-being.	**Quadrant 4:** High Wisdom, High Compassion Wise Compassion. Leaders combine strategic insight and effective decision-making with genuine care and empathy for all employees in need of assistance.

The *Harvard Business Review* addressed this issue in a Dec. 4, 2020, article on leadership and managing people titled *"Compassionate Leadership Is Necessary — but Not Sufficient"* written by Rasmus Hougaard, Jacqueline Carter and Nick Hobson.

Their point is this: Compassion alone does not suffice for effective leadership. It must be paired with wisdom. As a leader, wisdom encompasses leadership skills, a profound grasp of what drives people and the know-how to manage them to achieve set objectives. Leadership is challenging. It frequently involves driving initiatives, providing difficult feedback, making tough choices which might upset people and sometimes necessitate layoffs. Compassionate leadership should not sacrifice wisdom and effectiveness. Both are essential. Wise compassionate leadership involves managing difficult situations in a humane manner.

Wise Compassion Quadrant Design

The Wise Compassion Quadrant, also known as the Wise Compassion Matrix, is a leadership framework combining wisdom and compassion to enhance leadership effectiveness and foster a positive work environment. This model is particularly valuable in guiding leaders to balance empathy with practical decision-making.

Below is a detailed explanation of the Wise Compassion Quadrant found on page 200:

Quadrant 1:

Indifferent and Ineffective (Low Wisdom, Low Compassion)

Characteristics: Leaders in this quadrant show neither compassion nor wisdom. They are often disengaged, make poor decisions, and do not connect with their team.

Impact: Results in low employee morale, high turnover, and poor organizational performance.

Quadrant 2:

Compassionate but Ineffective (Low Wisdom, High Compassion)

Characteristics: Leaders exhibit high empathy and care for their employees but lack the strategic insight and decision-making ability to lead effectively.

Impact: While the work environment might feel supportive, the organization may struggle with performance and achieving goals.

Quadrant 3:

Wise but not compassionate (High Wisdom, Low Compassion)

Characteristics: Leaders are skilled and knowledgeable, making effective decisions, yet lack empathy and concern for the team's well-being.

Impact: Can lead to short-term performance gains yet often results in long-term issues like burnout, low job satisfaction and high turnover.

Quadrant 4:

Wise Compassion (High Wisdom, High Compassion)

Characteristics: Leaders combine strategic insight and effective decision-making with genuine care and empathy for their employees.

Impact: This quadrant represents the ideal leadership style, leading to high employee engagement, loyalty, performance, and overall organizational success.

Developing Wise Compassion

To develop wise compassion, leaders should cultivate the following four skills:

Caring Presence: Definition: Being fully attentive and engaged with team members, showing genuine interest and concern. Practice: Active listening, being present in conversations, and showing empathy.

Caring Courage: Definition: Having the bravery to make tough decisions that may be uncomfortable but necessary. Practice: Addressing issues head-on, giving honest feedback, and making difficult calls with empathy.

Caring Candor: Definition: Communicating openly and honestly while maintaining respect and empathy. Practice: Providing clear and constructive feedback, being transparent about decisions and changes.

Caring Transparency: Definition: Being open and clear about intentions, decisions, and actions to build trust. Practice: Sharing information openly, explaining the reasons behind decisions, and being honest about uncertainties.

It is no accident I prefer to place wisdom ahead of compassion. Making wisdom a priority leaves room for compassion. Many times, taking time to be compassionate takes away some of the tools a leader needs to use while also limiting some of the actions they might need to take.

ANTICIPATORY LEADERSHIP

Remember, as leaders, you're not just leading today; you're architecting tomorrow. You're not just reacting to what hits you; you're sculpting the future with your vision. That's the power of anticipatory leadership. In a world that's constantly throwing curveballs, anticipating things is never a luxury. It should be your survival code.

Here are some powerful points, drawn straight from the cutting edge of leadership, designed to make anticipatory leadership the game-changer you need it to be:

Embrace the Inevitable: Disruption is the new normal. Stop treating change as a temporary inconvenience. The future isn't a straight line. It's a landscape of constant upheaval.

This quote hammers the concept home:

"Disruption isn't an anomaly;
it's the very fabric of our evolving world."

Roger Spitz

Leaders who understand this concept are rarely caught off guard because they're already strategizing for the next big wave.

Cultivate Your Sixth Sense: Relentlessly develop future capabilities. You can't predict the future, however, you can surely prepare for a multitude of them. This isn't about crystal balls. It is about systematic horizon scanning and identifying those faint signals of change with an understanding of their potential tsunami-like impact.

Build a culture of foresight within your organization: Leaders understand they are always on the line so they build strong cultures and systems. They anticipate the future so they can respond quickly and flexibly. They understand the unknown will happen . If the leader uses scenario thinking and prepares in advance to bounce back when a challenge presents, they will prosper when others withdraw.

All nonprofits went through tremendous shock when COVID hit our world. Some of them grew stronger while others failed or have yet to regain their footing.

During COVID, our organization set three all-time records in recruiting foster parents. In a time when many of the world's nonprofits faced challenges communicating with clients, we continued to communicate with our people and learned how to surmount the barriers imposed by the pandemic. These skills served us well because we learned them prior to the pandemic. We created ways our current families and those potential foster parents who wanted to continue serving children were still able to do so.

In the business world, some of the greatest organizational changes are created during the worst economic conditions. This can be done only through anticipating the most likely problems. Anticipatory leadership is about seeing around corners, preparing for future economic shifts and detecting emerging opportunities. Agility is the necessary key to your capacity in adapting swiftly and effectively to ever-changing circumstances. Agility bridges your long-term vision with the need for decisive current action.

Master the Art of What If: Leaders will benefit their organization most by leveraging the clues they are receiving about the future while planning scenarios for those things most likely to happen.

Great anticipatory leaders are scenario architects. They map out multiple plausible futures, stress-test their strategies against each, then develop robust plans to navigate any eventuality. This proactive approach is your shield against being blindsided.

Challenge your biases and assumptions: Flexibility and adaptability are necessary for your future growth. You don't need to be a perfect leader. However, it is necessary to make decisions correctly more often than not. One way to accomplish this, challenge assumptions and biases because they are your biggest blind spots. The world and its people are complex. Leaders continually want the world to fit into a framework we can easily and comfortably understand. Most also want to eliminate ambiguity. In real life, however, people are increasingly exposed to unknowns.

Several years ago, I was consulting with a CEO and he called me with great agitation in his voice.

"One of my senior employees is not doing what I want him to do!" he lamented.

As I asked questions, the CEO built a convincing case about how he thought it necessary to be very firm with his senior employee.

I listened until he was done explaining, then asked, "What do you have this senior employee doing?"

The CEO told me this employee recently acquired the largest, most profitable contract the company ever landed. Also, this same employee was involved overseeing a very complex process in the CEO's company.

"Do you know why he hasn't completed the one thing you want him to do within the time line you set?" I asked.

"No," he answered.

The CEO suddenly realized how very valuable was this employee. Yet, the CEO assumed the employee wasn't getting some assigned tasks completed.

"The problem might be your's, not your employee's," I gently suggested.

The CEO looked at his biases and assumptions and realized he was creating the tension and bringing his own mindset to a situation which required better understanding and a more courageous conversation about balancing initiative with priorities.

The CEO came away with a fresh paradigm. He and his senior employee began working together on projects by setting firm guidelines designed to help each of them to achieve more through cooperation. With a new perspective and a different mindset, the CEO was finally able to take effective action.

Anticipatory leaders cultivate cognitive flexibility, constantly challenging their own beliefs by embracing ambiguity and adapting with lightning speed to the new information.

Decentralize and Conquer: Effective leaders empower autonomous decision-making within their organizations. Teach your people to think for themselves! In today's hyper-fast environment, waiting for a top-down decisions is often a death sentence. Anticipatory leaders build trust and empower their team members at all levels to make informed decisions quickly and autonomously. The more decisions made at a lower level, the more actionable intelligence a leader will receive from the external source. This acts as a real-time early warning response system.

Hear the Whispers of Change: Implement robust early warning systems. As a leader, it is imperative you receive early warnings of any problems from your financial people, your process staff and your professional staff. If you don't hear what's happening in your world or you continue to receive only weak signals, you cannot eliminate or mitigate those major disruptions coming your way tomorrow.

At a restaurant recently, I passed by a busy kitchen on my way to the bathroom when I noticed a sign posted on the wall. The sign read: "If anyone asks about their meal, you are to tell the manager immediately."

This sign was clearly intended for the front line employees and serving staff. Culturally, the restaurant was trying to deliver excellent service. The leader knew if a customer asks questions about a meal, management should receive this information. Develop and utilize effective early warning systems to detect even subtle shifts in the market, technology or customer behavior. This will buy a leader precious time in order to prepare and pivot.

Experiment and Learn: Cultivate a culture of innovation. Failure isn't the opposite of success. It's a crucial stepping stone. Anticipatory leaders foster a culture where experimentation is encouraged. Learning from both successes and failures is paramount. This iterative process fuels continuous improvement to keep you ahead of the curve.

Solve Tomorrow's Problems Today: Shift from reaction to proaction.

> *"The difference between a good leader*
> *and a great one is anticipation, not reaction."*

Craig Groeschel

Most big problems start as small ones long ignored or never noticed. Anticipatory leaders are problem-finders and problem-solvers who pounce on small issues before they explode into crises. They see potential problems on the horizon and act decisively to address them early.

This is about creating innovation through anticipation: Seeing a looming problem should signal the opportunity for innovation.

Stay Humble, Stay Sharp: Avoid the curse of overconfidence. Your past successes can be your future downfall. Overconfidence breeds complacency, hinders feedback and stifles innovation. Anticipatory leaders approach the future with humility, recognizing what they think they know might not be true. They remain lifelong learners, constantly asking questions and seeking diverse perspectives. This humility is the bedrock of accurate anticipation.

Black Swan Events: These are the low-probability, high-impact events which seem to come out of nowhere and force leaders to rewrite the rules. Traditional thinking often fails to account for them. This generally ends with catastrophic consequences. Leaders who don't understand this phenomenon fall prey to the illusion of predictability by assuming a stable and controllable world will remain so always. They build strategies based on past trends and fail to consider the outliers.

Anticipatory leaders, however, share a different relationship with uncertainty. In retrospect, these leaders understand black swans are not always visible. Often, signs were there yet dismissed or unseen by those with a rigid mindset. While these leaders don't try to predict the unpredictable, they do build resilient systems able to withstand and even benefit from such unforeseen shocks. They operate with a heightened awareness of a volatile complex environment, acknowledging the inherent unknowability also brings with it the potential for exponential and intersecting change.

For anticipatory leaders, scenarios are not about predicting a single future; they are about exploring a range of possibilities including those which seem unlikely. By rigorously examining different scenarios, including high-impact as well as low-probability ones, they develop a portfolio of responses which build organizational muscle for quick adaptability. They understand reliance solely on past data and linear projections is often a recipe for disaster in a world punctuated by black swans. They no longer assume the absence of evidence is evidence of the absence of danger.

Instead of being blindsided, anticipatory leaders cultivate a posture of preparedness. They focus on building adaptability, fostering cognitive flexibility and creating early warning systems able to catch even the faintest signals preceding a black swan event. They understand the cost of unpreparedness for the unpredictable far outweighs the effort of thoughtful scenario planning while building resilient systems.

In essence, anticipatory leadership is about moving beyond the comfort of the present and proactively shaping a future where your organization doesn't just survive disruption, it thrives on it. It's about embracing uncertainty, cultivating fcresight and building agile, resilient capabilities not just to navigate waves of change, but to ride them to new horizons. Now go out there and architect your tomorrow.

ABOUT THE AUTHOR

If I were inclined to put my life in perspective at this time, it would include elements of surprise, blessings and a relentlessness to become the best at what I do. Recently I was at a large gathering of nonprofit leaders and the question was asked by the moderator: "How many founders of organizations are in the room?"

I was expecting to look around and see one third of the people raising their hands. To my surprise, it was less than 10 percent. Twenty years ago, a similar group would likely comprise more than 80 percent founders. This is the way of life in today's world.

When I started directing a drug and alcohol program at a hospital in Redding, Calif., I was among the youngest leaders in the city.

Now, 40 years later, I am one of the oldest. I'm still going to work each day as I did in my 30s. Innovating and creating a better operation while serving youth and adults who need support going through their lives is my goal each day.

I started my first nonprofit and served in it for more than 25 years. I invested $14,000 of my own money. At that time, it was a scramble to come up with the capital. Today, the organization's annual revenue is more than $15 Million.

Our first year's revenue was less than $50,000. I thought our organization was going to go under many times during our first year. My friends talked me off the ledge of quitting to find a "real" job many times. I went without paychecks numerous times during those first years.

Today, our organization includes more than 100 employees. We operate in five northern California counties with a total of seven divisions, Intensive Services Foster Care, clinical mental health services,-coaching services with 5 Peaks, Specialty Mental Health Services, Enhanced Care Management as well as Transitional Housing serving former youths who have aged out of foster care after turning 18.

My proudest accomplishment is the development of leaders. I hired social workers, clinicians, former pastors, clerical employees and trained them to be leaders of multi-million-dollar divisions. During my years of leadership in nonprofits, I founded two nonprofits, co-founded another two and served on the boards of numerous nonprofits, a college and as a member of the Tehama County Juvenile Justice Commission on County Behavioral Services. I also served with and consulted for many nonprofits and at least one college regarding leadership and strategic planning.

Mike Logan

BULK ORDERS, SPEAKING ENGAGEMENTS

Free Assessments:

Thank you for purchasing *A Nonprofit Leader's Edge!*

In appreciation of your purchase, we have included **two free assessments**.

1. One free assessment you can do for your entire organization.
2. A second free assessment is for the leader of your organization.

Our hope is these two tools will provide you with an insightful view of your organization and yourself as leader!

To receive the free assessments contact us at: mikelogan.org

Bulk orders:

We realize many of you purchase books for your team when you find a book you think will change how they lead and add to their quality of life. We can send you more information when you contact us at mikelogan.org about favorable pricing for bulk orders.

Consulting and Speaking:

Mike Logan is often asked to provide Executive Coaching or invited to speak at events either virtually or in person. Please contact us at mikelogan.org for more information or to speak directly with Mike Logan or a member of his team.

Thank you so much for your leadership and continuing to make this a better world by what you do!

For bonus resources, bookings, and to leave a review, please scan the QR code below.

Alternatively, visit mikelogan.org directly in your web browser to access additional material.